SELF-

DISCOVERY

IN RECOVERY

D1545543

SELF-
DISCOVERY
IN RECOVERY

Abraham J. Twerski, M.D.

1817

A HARPER/HAZELDEN BOOK

Harper & Row, Publishers, San Francisco

New York, Cambridge, Philadelphia, St. Louis
London, Singapore, Sydney, Tokyo

Library of Congress Cataloging-in-Publication Data

Twerski, Abraham J.
  Self-discovery in recovery.

  Reprint. Originally published: Center City, MN: Hazelden, © 1984.
  "A Harper/Hazelden book."
  1. Alcoholism—Psychological aspects. 2. Alcoholics—Psychology. 3. Alcoholics—Rehabilitation. I. Title.
[HV5045.T93   1989]   616.86'107   88-45678
ISBN 0-06-255491-3 (pbk.)

89 90 91 92 93 MAPLE 10 9 8 7 6 5 4 3 2 1

This book is dedicated to
all the wonderful people in recovery
who have enriched my life
by allowing me to share
their recoveries with them.

CONTENTS

INTRODUCTION

In treating alcoholics, I have become aware of Alcoholics Anonymous (A.A.) and am enamored with this program. I find the Twelve Steps of A.A. are not only helpful to the alcoholic, but can also be an excellent program for personality development of all persons, alcoholic or nonalcoholic, drinkers or nondrinkers.

Although I'm not an alcoholic, I believe I benefit greatly from my closeness to A.A. I feel much like the youngster who wins a free ticket to the movie, and enjoys the movie even more because he or she doesn't have to pay the admission price. I feel privileged to enjoy the rewards of A.A. without having had to pay the costly admission fee.

As a nonalcoholic writing for alcoholics, I always feel a lack of experience. My identification with the alcoholic is considerable, having been acquired through years of working with thousands of patients. Still, my identification can never be complete. There are moments when I regret, much to people's astonishment, that I'm *not* an alcoholic.

Many times I'm confronted with emotionally distraught patients for whom neither psychotherapy nor medication appears effective. I know many of these people could benefit greatly from the fellowship and the growth program of Alcoholics Anonymous, but since they don't have a drinking or other chemical problem, they can't identify with the people in the program.

1

My bias toward A.A. is thus perceived. It's a dangerous over-generalization to say A.A. is the *only* resource necessary to help alcoholics with their problems. Even with recovery from alcoholism, other aspects of a person's life, physical, social, psychological, and spiritual, may require additional attention.

Abstinence from alcohol and from the lifestyle characteristic of the alcoholic are the essentials for recovery. A holistic approach to the entire person is required for achieving the greatest potential of recovery.

To that end this book is directed.

CHAPTER I

BEAUTIFUL PEOPLE

A young woman sits in the hospital lounge biting her lip, and tries in vain to fight back the tears that stream down over her black and blue eyes. She can't recall how she got the bruises, whether in a drunken brawl or by falling, her equilibrium thrown off by alcohol and pills. Such blackouts aren't new to her; even though she is only 22, she has experienced many such amnesic episodes.

Barbara isn't crying because of the bruises; these too have become commonplace. She's crying because, in spite of her patchy memory, she remembers her mother threw her out of the house, with instructions never to return. She had come home with two men whom she befriended at the bar, and when the guys refused to leave, mother called the police. When Barbara was freed at the police station, she had no place to go, and the police brought her to the hospital.

Barbara's adventures with alcohol began at age 13, initially with beer. Then came marijuana, "ludes," speed, hard liquor, "percs," valium, and whatever else happened to be available.

"Tell me," I said, "What do you do when you work around the kitchen and you accumulate garbage?"

"I don't understand what you mean," Barbara said.

"Just what I said." I repeated, "Where do you put the garbage that you accumulate?"

"Why, in the garbage can," she replied. "Where else?"

"Then I have only one question for you, Barbara. If you know the only place for garbage is the garbage can, why did you put all that garbage into yourself?"

Barbara forced a smile. "I guess I wanted to get high."

"No way," I said. "You knew this stuff was garbage. I'm sure of that. I believe your self-concept was so distorted, you didn't consider yourself to be anything but a garbage can, and that's why you took all that junk. If you believed you were the beautiful person you really are, you never could have done that to yourself. When you have something you consider to be of value, you take care of it. If you have something beautiful, you polish it and protect it; you don't batter it carelessly."

Barbara nodded her head slowly. "I never thought I was any good," she said.

So it is with Barbara and thousands of others. So it was with Paul, who never came out of his room while in detox, and never allowed his eyes to meet anyone else's. He was petrified that if anyone came close to him they would somehow smell the rot he felt inside him; and that if anyone looked into his eyes, they would see through him and discover a cesspool. But Paul is a beautiful person, and so is Barbara, and so are the thousands of others. Beautiful people blind to their true self-worth. Beautiful people who see themselves as being hideous.

I don't know the cause of alcoholism, and I am most skeptical of anyone who does claim to know *the* cause. Maybe there are hundreds of different causes, just as there are hundreds of varieties of alcoholism. But I do know something for certain. In my experience, I have never come across an alcoholic who had a positive sense of self-worth, feelings of adequacy and self-confidence, *prior to becoming involved with alcohol.* The feelings of being "different" from others, of being less than others, whether less attractive, less intelligent, less personable, less charismatic, less energetic, or perhaps all of the above, were characteristic of alcoholics even before the drinking overtook their lives.

An alcoholic who is celebrating his twenty-fifth anniversary of sobriety puts it this way:

"I remember feeling inferior to others. Everybody had something I didn't have. And there were times when I felt superior to others. I degraded people, and I looked down upon them with contempt. But I never felt equal to others, except when I drank. Alcohol was the great equalizer. Whether you're above others or beneath them, you're alone and you're lonely, and that is miserable, because you don't belong. I wanted to belong, and alcohol gave me that feeling."

Why then, can we not say feelings of low self-worth are the *cause* of alcoholism? Simply because there are countless people with feelings of inferiority or inadequacy who don't become alcoholic. Many find other ways of dealing with these feelings, some more destructive, some less destructive, and some even constructive but at a high cost. Some, ideally, overcome the distorted self-concepts and discover themselves to be positive people rather than negative.

Low self-esteem is *not* the cause of alcoholism, but a facet of the alcoholic's personality that can be overcome and must be overcome if abstinence is to grow into true sobriety, and if life without alcohol is to be the gratifying experience that it can be.

CHAPTER II

PRE-DRINKING INFERIORITY

"But of course," you will say. "How do you expect an alcoholic not to have poor self-esteem? How much self-esteem can you get from waking up in the local drunk tank, or in a prison cell after being arrested for disorderly conduct? Getting reprimands at work or losing your job doesn't do much for self-esteem, nor does waking up with a hangover. And having your wife berate you day after day isn't exactly ego-edifying either."

There is no question that the consequences of alcoholic drinking are harmful and universally degrading. The problem of low self-esteem that we are going to discuss is not that which occurs *after* the drinking, but those feelings of self-consciousness, social awkwardness, and fear of failure that *preceeded* the drinking. When we observe the physical, social, and emotional damages from drinking, we may find it difficult to believe there were feelings of low self-worth prior to the drinking. But if we observe alcoholism in its early stages, what some prefer to call "problem-drinking," we will see that negative self-image exists prior to the consequences of drinking. Furthermore, an adequate history obtained from those who knew the alcoholic before he or she drank will reveal obvious signs of low self-esteem that existed even then.

In the previous chapter, a recovering alcoholic said the

only time he felt equal to others was when he drank. This feeling is not uncommon. Many alcoholics say, "I have to drink to feel normal," and by this they do not mean only needing alcohol to suppress the tremors and the heart palpitations, although this certainly occurs. What they are referring to is if they drink alcohol they feel "average," and without it they feel unequal. The alcoholic may not necessarily be drinking in order to get "high," but merely to feel "equal."

The statement, "I either felt inferior to others or superior to them," really represents two sides of the same coin. Feelings of inferiority may be so intolerable that the person sometimes escapes from this misery by fantasizing to be superior to others, and then adopts an air of condescension, a trait often found in the active alcoholic particularly during intervals of abstinence. This fantasy of superiority may be initiated or reinforced by the degradation of others. The person is hypercritical of others, constantly finding fault with them, accentuating their faults or mistakes and belittling their virtues or accomplishments. Indeed, this behavior of tearing others down may go away when the person becomes intoxicated. For then alcohol brings on the "equal" feelings and the person no longer needs to bring others down to his or her level. Active alcoholics with this pattern are often said to be "impossible when dry."

This tendency to fantasize one's self as superior to others in order to escape from painful feelings of inferiority is not unique to the alcoholic. This same trait is frequently found in nonalcoholics as well. We all know people who boast of themselves and who belittle everyone else. The importance of this in understanding its role in the alcoholic personality is twofold. (1) Like many other traits, it may be intensified many times over in the alcoholic. (2) And most important, overcoming this trait is an integral part of the alcoholic's recovery.

The feelings of inferiority are just that: they are feelings and nothing more. These feelings of inadequacy and inferiority the alcoholic has prior to drinking are distortions and misconceptions, not true facts. The person feels inadequate even though he is in reality very adequate; the person feels socially awkward, although she is in fact very sociable; the person feels unlikable or unlovable even though others may consider her quite charming and desirable. Of course, once the alcohol begins to exert its harmful effects, the person may indeed become all those negative things or fantasies. This is the phenomenon of the self-fulfilling prophesy. The people who feel inferior, and drink to escape those feelings of inferiority, may drink themselves into actually being inferior, and then say, "See, I told you before, no one likes me and no one wants me."

There is something even more tragic about the distorted self-concept that causes unwarranted feelings of inferiority; such feelings are apt to be more intense in persons who are gifted and who are in reality capable and competent. A study of alcoholic physicians, for example, revealed the overwhelming majority to have graduated in the upper one-third of their classes.

Why is this so? The phenomenon is a fact whether or not one can explain it, but I like to think about it as follows:

Somewhere in the person's development, often in the early or formative years of life, something happens that causes a distorted self-concept. This distortion often consists of seeing oneself as the reverse of reality, a condition I call "negative self-image." Just as in photography, what is darkest in the negative appears brightest on the print, so with the negative self-image.

Assume we have some way of objectively evaluating people according to their personality assets: intelligence, appearance, charisma, temperament, assertiveness, and innate talents; and that we can grade people as ranging from 0 to +10, based on their having varying degrees of these personality ingredients. Now suppose that a person who has a rating of +3 develops a distorted self-concept. Since this person sees herself as the reciprocal of what she is *in fact*, she will feel like a rating of −3. On the other hand, imagine the person whose excellence is such that objectively he would be rated a +10. If this person develops a distorted self-concept and sees himself as the reciprocal, he will consider himself a −10. Hence, the phenomenon that very intense feelings of low self-esteem are apt to be found in the most gifted people.

Recognition of this phenomenon will help us understand some of the most bewildering and unfathomable behavior of the alcoholic, and also why there is much reason for optimism even in the alcoholic who appears intensely self-destructive.

In the pages that follow, the term "negative self-image" will refer to a person who has feelings of inadequacy and inferiority. Low self-esteem and lack of self-confidence are thus the consequences of the person's distorted self-perception. Yet, because a person generally trusts his or her own senses, the person with a negative self-image acts as though the perceived negativity is reality.

CHAPTER III

FALLING UP THE STAIRS

One often hears a recovering alcoholic describe the phenomenon of "falling *up* the stairs." Everybody else, the recovering alcoholic will say, falls down the stairs.

What is being referred to is the drinking alcoholic's ability to advance in job or business, make more money than ever, get promotions and awards for distinction, civic honors, and recognition of various types while his or her life falls apart. It is almost universally believed that the last thing to go is one's work performance. Family life deteriorates, social life may be in ruins, one's emotions become chaotic, but satisfactory job performance can remain intact until very late in the illness.

I know of an excellent surgeon who performed a kidney transplant, a highly-complex piece of surgery, with flawless technique. The patient did extremely well, without any complications. On the day following surgery, the surgeon made his rounds with a group of residents, interns, and medical students surrounding him. As they approached the patient's bed, the chief resident said, "This is Mr. Smith, Doctor, and he is doing quite well."

"Who the hell is Smith?" the doctor asked.

"He is the patient on whom you did the kidney transplant yesterday," the resident answered. "His vital signs are good, and his urinary output is adequate."

"You must be out of your mind," the surgeon said. "I didn't do any kidney transplant yesterday."

This is a perfect example of how even work that requires great concentration and precision can be successfully performed in the advanced stages of alcoholism.

The person with a negative self-image may try to overcome painful feelings of inferiority by demonstrating how successful he or she can be. In this way, the person tries to prove to others—spouse, parents, family, friends—that he or she is not inadequate and incompetent. More than all else, the person tries to prove this to him- or herself. Never mind that others may already think highly of him or her. The person is convinced that everyone else is aware of this inferiority, too.

Case No. 1

Oliver was 57 when he sought psychiatric help because of an alcohol problem.

Oliver recalled as a youngster he felt extremely bad about himself. He was rejected by his father, and for reasons that are unclear, he felt ashamed of his mother. He decided early in life that he would make a name for himself.

Oliver was very bright, and worked his way through college and entered law school. He married while in college and held several jobs simultaneously to support his family. He took a job with a corporation and advanced to a high executive position. In spite of repeated demonstrations of his skill and capabilities, Oliver always lived in fear that his inadequacies would be discovered and he would be fired. Even when he reached top executive level, he dreaded every presentation to the board of directors, thinking he'd be criticized.

It is not clear at what point Oliver's drinking began, but it led to the termination of his marriage. What brought him to the psychiatrist was the deterioration of the marriage. Although he confided that he no longer loved his wife, the feeling that he was a failure in marriage was intolerable. His drinking had at this time not affected his work, and his feeling that the marriage failure revealed a personality defect spurred him on to heightened productivity at work.

The negative self-image person may thus be very energetic and productive, since the person is incessantly driven by the need to prove him- or herself. However, one can never compensate for a deficiency that exists only in the person's fantasy. Delusions are not amenable to either logical argument or contradiction by reality. If a psychotic person believes he or she is the messiah, you can't argue this belief or successfully prove otherwise. Similarly, the person with a delusion of inferiority will not change his or her self-concept when he or she succeeds at something, no matter what the magnitude of achievement. At the very best, the achievement will give the person a brief period of satisfaction, but the person will promptly set out to prove him- or herself once again.

If the negative self-image person is alcoholic, he or she will, as mentioned earlier, begin to suffer some consequences of drinking in personal life. These will further depress self-esteem; and if the method of overcoming feelings of inferiority is to prove him- or herself in the marketplace, the person will intensify these efforts while self-esteem progressively suffers from personal setbacks. In other words, the alcohol-induced failures in personal life may become the stimuli for increased assertiveness in business life. Inasmuch as work performance is not affected by alcohol until near the end, the person may indeed continue to further him- or herself, achieving all the rewards of the increased efforts. When the drinking begins interfering with work performance, thus taking away the only trace of self-esteem, everything comes down like a house of cards. This final failure is apt to bring about depression and a total abandon of all emotions.

CHAPTER IV

COPING vs. ESCAPING

Many people drink to escape. Alcohol is a powerful tranquilizer, or perhaps better yet, an anesthetic. Alcohol can make one oblivious to everything in the world. While not everyone who drinks to escape necessarily becomes alcoholic, escapist drinking carries a high risk of developing into alcoholism. At any rate, it certainly is characteristic of many alcoholics to drink to escape.

When you come right down to it, there are only two possible reactions to any challenge: coping or escaping. Obviously, escaping isn't always inappropriate. If you find yourself in your car stalled on the railroad tracks, and you see a train coming toward you at 120 miles an hour, it would be crazy to waste time in deciding what to do. The tragic result would be one dead, foolish "coper." Common sense tells you that the thing to do is get out of that car quickly; escape is the only sensible and proper response.

However, let me share with you a radio commercial I heard several years ago. It went something like this:

"Oh, Grace, what am I to do? My husband has invited his boss home for dinner, and my sink drain is clogged."

"You poor thing," Grace responds. "You should take some aspirin."

"I don't have a headache," the lady says. "I'm just so upset and tense."

"Well, if that's how you feel, you should take _____"
(a tranquilizer), Grace suggests.

Following this dialogue, the announcer explains the
wonderful tranquilizing effects of this particular drug.

As a sophomore medical student, I had an instructor
who taught, "Never prescribe medication unless you have
first identified the presence of an illness. All medications
are chemicals which can affect the body tissues, and some
side effects may be very serious. The only justification for
introducing a chemical into the body is when an illness
presents a greater danger to the person than any possible
harmful effect of the medication. But if there is no illness,
then no medication is justified."

This appears to be so elementary and so logical that it
need hardly be said. Yet, the most widely-used medications
in the United States (whether prescribed by a physician
or the over-the-counter type) are tranquilizers and sedatives, like the one in the radio ad. Is the lady who is nervous
or uptight really sick? Has every physician who prescribes
a tranquilizer identified a real illness? We all know being
tense, nervous, or uptight is unpleasant, but is every un-
pleasantness in life an illness? If the principle of "no
illness—no medication" were observed, how many pre-
scriptions for tranquilizers and sedatives would be eliminated?

Getting back to the radio commercial, let's look for the
presence of an illness. We'll start with the husband who
invited the boss for dinner. Several weeks before, the husband may have explained it to his wife like this:

"Honey," he said, "this is the break we've been waiting
for. I could get the promotion and an increase in salary, a
more liberal expense account, increased commissions, and
a chance for even better promotions. I've been with this
firm for fourteen years, and I've got a good sales record. I
think I've got a good crack at that job.

"But you know the boss has this thing about corporate
image. Everyone in a managerial position has to wear a

three-piece suit with a handkerchief in the breast pocket. You have to reflect stability. Look, honey, I'll invite the boss for dinner; he'll have a chance to see our home, the pictures of the kids, how we live, and you'll put on one of your special dinners. I tell you, that job is as good as mine."

Of course, the wife was equally thrilled. However, in preparation for the great event the sink backs up. You can't prepare an elaborate meal without access to a functioning sink, and so our lady becomes tense, anxious, uptight. In desperation, she turns to Grace.

Is the lady's reaction an illness? Wouldn't anyone in this predicament become tense and anxious? She may be uneasy, but if this isn't an illness, why take medication?

If Grace would have used good judgment, she would have said, "Relax. I'll hop in my car and be back in ten minutes with a can of drain cleaner and a plunger, and we'll get that sink drain open in no time at all."

However, this wasn't Grace's response. Instead, what she essentially said was, "Don't worry about a clogged sink drain. Take some tranquilizers, and you'll forget about it." Grace's message is that of alcoholism and addiction: Got a problem? Zonk yourself with a chemical and you'll forget about it. Unfortunately, problems not dealt with effectively don't go away when one chooses to be oblivious to their existence. All alcoholics and addicts have learned this very painful and costly lesson.

Let's continue with our scenario. As Grace suggests, the woman takes some tranquilizers. After a bit she feels fine and is no longer anxious, tense, or upset. She continues preparing her elaborate dinner, and eventually the sink overflows. As the tranquilizing effects of the pills wear off, she is now confronted with a disaster. Not only does she have a clogged sink drain, but now she has a messy kitchen floor with the water beginning to make its way into the dining room.

"Where is that bottle of pills?" she cries. She decides

she'll need at least twice what she took before. After downing four tranquilizers, the lady is once again at ease.

At six o'clock, just when the effect of the tranquilizers is at its peak, the husband brings his boss home to show him their serene home life, their stability and reliability. He opens the door to see water everywhere, and his wife dancing and singing at the top of her voice. The husband quickly pulls the door shut, "Sorry, b-b-boss," he stammers. "There's been an accident. Let's go to a restaurant." You can imagine how little the husband enjoys his dinner.

When our man returns home, the effects of the tranquilizers have worn off, and the wife, confronted with the chaos in the house and the awareness of how she ruined their golden opportunity, sits in total dejection. The husband lets loose his pent-up wrath with the force of a volcanic eruption. The wife runs up to the bedroom and grabs the bottle of pills. But this time, not even four are enough. The whole bottle, and she'll be at peace forever.

What we have done here is condense the course of chemical dependency into a few hours. The usual course may take years, but the outcome is much the same. Problems that are ignored don't go away, they get worse. And if we continue to ignore the problems, they compound themselves many times over, and the ultimate escape is not too far away.

We thus have two distinct examples of reacting to challenges. The first is the oncoming train, where there is universal agreement that escape is proper; and the second is the clogged sink drain, where everyone will certainly agree that getting the drain unclogged would have been the proper action, rather than popping pills. What makes escape proper in one situation and not in the other? When is coping the correct reaction, and when is it inappropriate?

It is important to know how to make the correct response. We are bombarded by challenges all our waking life. At work, with the family, socially, as a community citizen; there are challenges everywhere.

The A.A. program teaches, "keep it simple." This is nowhere better applied than here. The simple rule is, if the challenge is much bigger than you, then turn it over to your Higher Power. If you are bigger than the challenge, take care of it and resolve it. If you seem to be rather evenly matched, call someone to help you.

Since the formula is so simple, why have so many people's lives been ruined because of escapist maneuvers? Why aren't more people coping effectively rather than escaping?

The answer to this is also quite simple. The evaluation of any challenge confronting me has two components: the challenge and myself. I must judge how big the challenge is and then I must assess how big I am. After I have made these two determinations, I can apply the "keep it simple" formula.

Whether I decide to cope or escape depends a great deal on how I assess myself, particularly my strengths and capabilities; based on how I see myself, not what I *am*. If I see myself as weak, incompetent, and unintelligent, I will likely choose escape often, because I will see challenges as being beyond my coping capabilities. The poorer my self-concept is, the more escapist I am likely to be.

Since some of the most intense negative self feelings occur in gifted people, the phenomenon of super-people ruining their lives with alcohol can be better understood. According to their distorted self-concept, everything confronting them is overwhelming. Criticized by the boss? Go for a drink. Pressured to complete a project? Go for a drink. Bills are due? Where's that six-pack? School principal says son is caught with marijuana? Go out and tie one on.

All this is compounded by the fact that medicinal use of alcohol will eventually further depress one's self-esteem. And as the self-esteem becomes progressively depressed, the original response of escapism increases in frequency and intensity.

Many recovering alcoholics believe they must distinguish between being dry and being sober. As one puts it, "If the problem were alcohol, the solution would be simple: stop drinking! But the problem isn't alcohol; it's alcoholism. It's the rotten, miserable feeling you get when you don't drink, and it's so intolerable that you have to drink simply to survive."

I've presented this discussion of coping vs. escaping to people in treatment. One woman wrote,

> Just had to write and let you know how my new year began. I had all my in-laws over for dinner on New Year's Day. I prepared everything myself, but I was still very insecure about my ability.
>
> While in treatment I had the good fortune twice to hear your lecture on the radio commercial with Grace and the tranquilizers. I knew that would never happen to me. I never once had a clogged sink drain in fifteen years of marriage.
>
> Well, guess what!?! I was busy preparing the big meal when I realized I was standing in an inch of water. I bent down under the sink, yet looked up to find the source of all this water. I came out from under the sink all smiles. I realized for the first time I could bend down and look up at the same time without the dizziness of a hangover. I also remembered the radio commercial and knew I had a problem to face. I was stronger than the sink drain, and I thanked God this hadn't happened before I'd been through treatment.
>
> My husband tried all day but couldn't clear the drain. I'd have to fix my dinner with no sink! I didn't panic and took constructive action. I drained vegetables, etc., in the bathroom and after dinner, washed all the dishes downstairs in the laundry tub. The old me would never have coped! But I knew I could do it with help and willingly accepted it. As a result, we all had a good laugh at the situation and became closer because of it.

This turned out to be the best holiday season in years, thanks to the program and your lecture.
Happy New Year and God bless!

Gratefully, Mary L.

Mary was fortunate to recognize early in her recovery that she had the capacity to deal constructively with a big problem. Because she had chosen to cope, everyone enjoyed an experience of mutual help, and what would have been a devastating failure in her drinking days turned out to be highly successful in sobriety.

CHAPTER V

ORIGINS OF LOW SELF-ESTEEM

How do we get negative self-images? One might think that the person who developed unwarranted low self-esteem would be the product of an unhappy childhood with parents who were neglectful or abusive. Or that the person grew up under circumstances of deprivation, was orphaned early, and had a wicked stepmother or serious illnesses in childhood, or whose most prominent memory is a father yelling, "You're a rotten kid. You'll never grow up to amount to anything!" However, we find many alcoholics and nonalcoholics with negative self-image problems who appear to have had normal homes without any evidence of gross physical or emotional suffering in childhood.

We might look at it this way. Human beings come into the world with two strikes against them. Of all living things, we are the most helpless and the most dependent on our parents for survival for the longest time, while undoubtedly also being the most sensitive. Being helpless and dependent depresses one's self-esteem, and so we learn early to assert ourselves.

This struggle for self-assertion can be seen even in infants. Any mother with a baby several months old can tell you there is a struggle for mastery. The mother's attempt to feed the child may be countered by the child's clamping his or her mouth shut in defiance. When the mother somehow manages to get a spoonful of food into the baby's mouth, he or she may just sit there with it and refuse to swallow. The baby may do this even though he or she is hungry, proven by the fact that if mother is called away to the phone, the child eats everything in sight. What had been going on was clearly a battle of the wills, with the baby trying to be assertive even at this tender age.

Another classic struggle of wills occurs during toilet training. A mother can go crazy from the constant frustration at her child's refusal to evacuate in the toilet, only to fill the diaper within minutes of being taken off the toilet. The defiance against mastery by others thus begins at an early age.

I recall when my oldest son was two years of age; he would refuse to let us put on his coat. He would grab it from us, pull away, and say, "No, no. Me!", then proceed to put it on upside down and backwards.

At that time, I didn't realize that he was a little person living in a grossly adult world. He had little independence. He was put into bed and taken out of bed. He went outside when we wished and was brought in when we wished. He generally could eat only what we thought he should have, rather than what he wanted. In this totally big-people oriented and adult-dominated world, he asserted his sense of being by rejecting help and saying, "I can do it myself."

Does this sound familiar? Many alcoholics, prior to recovery, go through an extended period where they refuse any assistance and insist they can do things by themselves. Whether one has a sense of littleness because one is in fact little, or because one feels little, is all the same. Perhaps the low self-esteem in the adult is the feeling of littleness in childhood that was never overcome.

Outgrowing the sense of littleness and maturing into an emotionally healthy adult with a sound ego is not easily accomplished. When circumstances in the child's formative years permit healthy growth, the emerging personality has a healthy ego. When things happen that interfere with healthy growth, the adult personality is apt to have problems of adjustment, possibly alcoholism, neurotic traits, or psychosomatic illnesses.

Realization of one's capabilities can occur when a child successfully tests his or her strengths. The child wishes to do something, makes the effort at doing it, and accomplishes the goal. This allows the child to become aware of his or her abilities and to feel good about using them effectively.

There is a rather narrow margin in which this can be accomplished. If parents are overprotective or overindulgent, and do so much that the child doesn't get adequate opportunity to do things alone, he or she doesn't have sufficient testing of abilities and doesn't get to know his or her strengths. On the other hand, if parents demand some type of performance before the child has the ability to successfully perform, the child may develop a sense of failure and futility, and believe he or she doesn't have the capacity to achieve what should be achieved. Successful parenting is like walking a tightrope, where leaning too far to one side is as bad as leaning too far to the other.

In addition to parents, other significant people and peers in a child's life may be of considerable influence. Grandparents, aunts, and uncles can affect a child by showing preference for another child in the family. Teachers can also exert powerful influences over a child. A sensitive child who feels humiliated in front of peers may feel too threatened to ever try any self-assertion again.

Numerous incidents, many beyond the control of parents, can slow the development of a positive self-image. Absence of either parent may affect the child, since desertion by a parent can be taken to mean that the child is somehow bad. Although the absence may be explained, military service, a prolonged illness, etc., a young child is not able to grasp these fine points. The child may then interpret the absence as desertion and feel that he or she is bad. Parental preoccupation with a sibling who may require a great deal of attention because of illness or other problems may be interpreted by the well child as a preference for the other. Being surpassed by a sibling, particularly by a younger one, may result in grossly exaggerated feelings of inferiority.

Some cultural factors can also inhibit self-esteem development. The comfort and support of a peer group is a positive feature, while being an outsider causes negative feelings. Families who relocate several times because of job transfers, etc., repeatedly subject the young children to being outsiders to a new group. The parents' own security and adjustment are strained by repeated relocations, and this filters down to the children. Prior to our super-industrialized society, families lived in the same community and even in the same home for generations. Being this firmly rooted in the community enhanced everyone's sense of security. The lack of such durable relationships causes many problems for a sense of security and self-esteem. Urban overcrowding, mechanization, and mass production also subtract from the sense of uniqueness and individuality essential for a sense of personal significance.

The negative self-image is thus a product of the way we all begin our lives, and it takes an ideal set of circumstances to overcome this and develop a positive sense of being. Since the ideal is rarely reached, the persistence of the negative self-image into adulthood is frequent. As we shall see, there are numerous ways people try to cope with life based on their misconceptions of themselves, and unfortunately, many of these reinforce the negative self-image rather than overcome it. Whenever the factors that render a person vulnerable to alcoholism exist, the complicated syndrome of alcoholism emerges including the characteristic self-disapproval and self-depreciation. And it becomes even more difficult to overcome a negative self-image.

For many alcoholics, a behavior pattern exists which some people refer to as "fear of success." This is characterized by a repetitious use of energy to achieve a particular goal, but when the person is just within reach of achievement, he or she does something to cause failure. Generally that "something" is a heavy drinking spree, filled with self-destructive behavior.

I have difficulty accepting the "fear of success" theory. It seems to me that the desire for success is so universal that fear of success is illogical. In some cases I have found that what appears to be fear of success is in reality fear of failure.

Everyone has some fear of failure, and a fear of something unpleasant. Yet, we do things that have a risk of failure, with full knowledge that if we fail, it will be an unpleasant experience. However, if the risk involves one's total destruction or something like that, the risk is rarely taken.

To the person with a negative self-image, the thought of failure may be utterly devastating. The person's ego may be so frail that failure can't be tolerated. One way to avoid failure is to simply not try anything, based on the premise that if you don't try, you can't fail. The person who has this frame of mind may stay in bed long into the day, dilly-dally around, and find numerous excuses for not looking for a job or trying to make a sale. The person won't ask a friend for a date because he or she might be refused. If failure results from inaction it is explained by the fantasy that, "had I tried, I could have succeeded," and the person then believes there were circumstances that prevented him or her from taking action.

Where there is a profound negative self-image, the fear of failure is actually an anticipation of failure. The person is so convinced of inadequacy that failure is certain if he or she tries. The person is sure rejection or refusal will occur.

There are several times, however, when fear of failure doesn't slow an action until the person comes close to finishing the task. Then the fear or anticipation of failure gains in intensity, and the person may abort the project.

Anxiety that accompanies the waiting for an unpleasant event can be extremely difficult to tolerate. You've probably experienced this, in moderate form, in the dentist's waiting room. And the person who has a biopsy taken and must wait several days to learn whether or not cancer is present may experience very severe anxiety. The person whose ego is so frail that rejection or failure seems like a total attack on the personality may actually be unable to tolerate the suspense and anxiety of the anticipation. For this individual it may be easier to bring on failure and be done with it, since the person sees failure as inevitable. Many alcoholics are adept at this maneuver. Their lives are a series of events, each stopped before it could be successfully accomplished.

What appears to be "fear of success" can thus be understood as the reverse. It is often really anticipation of failure. It becomes evident why, in addition to abstinence from alcohol, changes in self-esteem are essential for recovery.

CHAPTER VI

PROVOCATIVE BEHAVIOR

Richie was 32 when he entered an alcoholism rehabilitation center. Almost half of his life had been spent in reformatories, jails, and state hospitals. When Richie's counselor referred him to the rehab program, I thought the counselor had flipped. I didn't think Richie could learn to live outside an institution. But Richie learned and it was uplifting to hear him talk about his illness and recovery when he was four years into sobriety.

At one point Richie asked, "Why did I drink? Who knows why. None of us know why we drank." Then after a brief pause he said in a rather soft tone, "Yeah, I know one reason why I drank. I wanted people to hate me because I was a drunk and not because I was Richie."

This observation, not an interpretation by a therapist, but a genuine expression of feeling by a person who remembers his torment and has the intuition to understand it, is filled with psychological wisdom.

A psychiatrist laid down a principle of psychology which explains much of human behavior including Richie's feelings. He said, "It is easier for a person to feel rejected because of what he *does* rather than because of what he *is.*"

Suppose a person feels despised by everyone for being a despicable person; i.e., that in every way, the person is horrible and repulsive. Since the person is convinced that the self is inherently bad, he or she believes there is no hope of ever being different or accepted.

If, however, a person believes he or she behaved in a manner that was offensive to others, and was shunned because people didn't like the behavior, all he or she has to do is discontinue the obnoxious behavior and acceptance can be found. Feeling rejected for what one *does* is much more tolerable than feeling rejected for what one *is*.

Human emotions and feelings are extremely clever. Just as the body has many automatic defense systems against disease which function without any awareness of their operation by the person, so our emotional systems have defense mechanisms which serve to protect us without our being aware anything is going on.

Assume a person believes no one likes him or her. Without adequate reason to explain the attitudes, the person would begin to believe there is something despicable about his or her very person. If, however, the attitudes toward the person were the result of an undesirable behavior, things would not be all that bad.

The psychological trick that takes place goes something like this. It is as though a little voice were telling the person, "Look, you'll feel much less miserable if you can attribute others' rejection of you to some obnoxious behavior. Go ahead and behave obnoxiously so you will have something to attribute the rejection to. Otherwise you are stuck with the conclusion that you are just plain despicable, and that's impossible to take." Of course, the person doesn't hear this little voice even as a silent thought process. The whole operation takes place without the person's awareness of what is going on. This is what Richie had observed about himself. This feeling is one of the consequences of a distorted self-concept, wherein the person who may in fact be very likeable cannot see himself this way.

Yet, Richie's observation is a most important one, because if drunkenness serves the purpose of alleviating the pain of rejection, then abstinence would very likely result in the person's adopting some other type of provocative behavior to explain the anticipated rejection. This is another reason why acquiring a positive self-esteem is essential in the recovery from alcoholism.

CHAPTER VII

ALCOHOLIC COURAGE

"I drink because it gives me courage." Not an unfamiliar statement, particularly in earlier phases of alcoholism. When the condition is far advanced one hardly feels like explaining the drinking any more than one would feel compelled to explain breathing. Before reaching this state, however, alcoholics often feel a drink gives them strength or ability to do things they could not do otherwise.

It is interesting to note who the people are who need alcohol for encouragement. A bank vice-president, whose financial and administrative skills enabled him to reach the position where he oversees twenty-seven of the bank's branches, has to have two stiff drinks before conducting the weekly meeting of the branch managers. A young woman who is stunningly attractive and very intelligent finds strength with alcohol before and during a date. A highly skillful surgeon who doesn't feel comfortable operating without an alcohol bracer. A lawyer who feels he can't argue his case before a jury without drinking. A priest who drinks in order to carry out his clerical duties. This phenomenon, where people look for self-confidence in a bottle, emphasizes the role of unjustified low self-esteem in alcoholism.

Alcohol is a central nervous system depressant. It is not, has never been, will never be, nor can it ever be anything else. Alcohol inhibits brain activity. It can't possibly make one more intelligent or more skillful.

Well, then, what about the people who are inactive or withdrawn who become lively and talkative after a few drinks? What about those people who *do* seem to function more efficiently after alcohol? If alcohol is a central nervous system depressant, then why does it sometimes appear to act as a stimulant?

There are some people who generally feel awkward and restrained, and alcohol, by anesthetizing the portions of the brain that control the inhibitions, removes these restraints. The people may feel more free to perform, but their performance is not what it would have been had they removed the restraints without drinking. This is because in the process of anesthetizing the brain, alcohol also depresses those brain cells that govern other aspects of the person's functioning. Depressed brain cells aren't as efficient as nondepressed brain cells. Compare the quality of function of the recovering alcoholic to that of his drinking days. Even if, in very early phases of the disease, the quality of performance doesn't appear affected while under the effects of alcohol, it isn't long before there's impairment of efficiency. Unfortunately, the nature of alcoholism is such that the alcoholic is oblivious to this deterioration.

The feelings which the alcoholic tries to drink away to feel comfortable are invariably products of the distorted self-image: feelings of inadequacy, incompetence, depression, anxiety, and self-consciousness.

Case No. 2

Frances is a Board Certified Pediatrician whose excellence enabled her to become the medical director of a facility. Frances recalls feeling self-conscious ever since her childhood. In her adolescence this resulted in total preoccupation with her weight, and she abstained from food in order to have a more presentable figure. She developed anorexia nervosa, a condition found in young women, where weight reduction goes totally out of control, resulting in radical weight loss and sometimes even in death. Frances' father, concerned about her alarming weight loss, encouraged her to drink beer for its calorie content. Frances quickly found the solution to her problem. Beer not only enabled her to eat, but also to feel comfortable enough to do many other things she thought impossible before.

Of course, Frances' distorted self-concept was hardly corrected by the beer, and it continued to manifest itself in many aspects of her life. For example, the man she chose to marry was clearly not in her league. Her parents had objected to the marriage, and her closest friends had said to her, "What is it that you see in Jim?" Although it was evident to all other observers that Jim was far inferior to Frances, her perception was such that Jim was an appropriate companion for her.

Fran managed to get through medical school and specialty training, switching somewhere along the way from beer to vodka. As the children began to come, she felt inadequate as a mother. Jim did everything he could to help her feel this way. Fran earned the money, worked hard as a doctor, and took care of the household, while Jim spent the money that she earned all the time telling her how rotten she was. Fran would fortify herself daily for her triple function with considerable amounts of alcohol.

When the morning tremors eventually developed, Fran was in a dilemma. She couldn't go to the office trembling like a leaf, yet she also knew that an odor of alcohol on her breath in the early morning hours would not be looked upon favorably in the hospital. It then occurred to her that the vanilla extract she used in baking contains alcohol, but would not smell like alcohol. She then began every day with a stiff drink of vanilla extract, and took along a bottle of vanilla extract in her purse to replenish her energy during the course of the day. Upon returning home, she would go back to the vodka.

The central nervous system depressant effects of alcohol

eventually made themselves known, and Fran was dismissed from her position. She was so depressed that she attempted suicide by overdosing with barbiturates, resulting in a three-day coma.

During her recovery in an alcoholism treatment center, Fran was noted to be not only depressed, but extremely down on herself. When her therapist asked her to list some of her personality strengths, Fran was unable to think of anything positive to say about herself.

The therapist then confronted Fran with some of the factual data in her record. "Look," he said. "You graduated from college and medical school. You completed training in your specialty. You graduated *Summa Cum Laude,* and you won the Phi Beta Kappa award. When I asked you to list any of your personality assets, you could at least have responded, 'Well, for whatever it's worth, I guess I'm not stupid. After all, I did achieve scholastic honors.' "

Fran sadly shook her head. "No," she said. "When they gave me the Phi Beta Kappa award, I knew they must have made a mistake."

The intensity of a negative self-image is so great it doesn't yield even in the face of contradiction by fact. This is one of the reasons why alcoholics who "fall *up* the stairs" are not reassured by their promotions or other acknowledgment of their achievements.

Case No. 3

Alan was a young man of 34 who admitted himself for detoxification at the insistence of his employer, who had previously warned him several times about his excessive drinking, and finally issued an ultimatum when Alan was found passed out one day at work.

Alan held a master's degree in science, and had an excellent job. His drinking began several years after his marriage, when he discovered that his sexual performance was inadequate, but that alcohol was an effective aphrodisiac.

It is of interest that Alan believed he was telling the gospel truth when he attributed his heavy drinking to his sexual inadequacy, although this would hardly account for his repeated drunkenness at work. Such absurd rationalizations and denial are subjects that merit discussion on their own.

The point in this case is that not too long after Alan began drinking to enhance sexual performance, his wife began rejecting him because she could not tolerate intimacy with a drunk. Needless to say, this rejection had the predictable consequence of Alan's increasing his drinking. At the time of his admission to the hospital Alan had been celibate for over a year. According to his own account, his wife had apparently not had any complaints about their sexual relationship until he began "improving" his performance with alcohol.

This is quite characteristic of the effects of alcohol when it is used to improve one's fantasized inadequacies. Although things begin to go to hell, the alcoholic somehow sees them as improving.

CHAPTER VIII
PASSIVITY AND ANGER

The desire of a person to be liked by others is universal and fundamental. There is probably no state of being that is as painful as isolation. Humans naturally crave closeness, and if a person withdraws from other people, it isn't because one doesn't crave closeness, but rather because one anticipates that any attempt at achieving intimacy will result in pain. This is much like having a beautiful rose, but it's never picked for fear of the pain the thorns might cause. Avoiding intimacy may also be from a preconviction that it is totally unattainable; i.e., an anticipation of rejection.

Both feelings, the fear of pain and the fear of rejection, generally arise from negative self-image delusion. People who feel inferior and inadequate are apt to consider themselves undesirable company to others. They can't see why others would want their friendship. Indeed, they are quite certain others would *not* want their friendship, and this conviction leads them to avoid attempts at intimate human contact. This is undoubtedly the dynamics of many alcoholic "loners."

This fear of rejection is operative in many aspects of an alcoholic's life. Notorious among these is management of anger and resentment. Harboring resentments is very destructive to the alcoholic, who generally deals poorly with all varieties of hostile feelings.

Hostile feelings of any type, whether hate, anger, envy, jealousy, or resentment, are generally unpleasant for anyone, and inappropriate attempts to deal with these feelings can result in maladaptations of various sorts. Difficulty in managing anger and resentment is prominent in people with low self-esteem.

The person who starts off with the premise that he or she is not liked by many people may be very frightened by feelings of anger. The person may feel that any manifestation of anger will alienate people, and since the person already feels impoverished in having so few human contacts, feelings of anger are a threat because they may deprive him or her of whatever human contact that has been retained.

Yet there is no way to avoid feelings of anger or resentment. Many things that are disturbing to us occur everyday, and these can make us angry. Other people may achieve what we have been unable to attain, and this can give rise to envy and resentment. People may say things, sometimes inadvertently and with no malice, that impinge upon our sensitivities and make us resentful. The person to whom such feelings are threatening is apt to suppress or repress them, in order to avoid further alienation.

Suppressed or repressed feelings do not lie dormant. They fester and churn inside us, as if fighting against the controls that deny their overt expression. The very tension generated by repressed feelings may contribute to drinking. Certainly, struggling with unresolved resentments is often a forerunner of a binge. Many recovering alcoholics know they must take their resentments to the nearest A.A. meeting and drop them off there, or else they're likely to drink.

If the person who is incapable of coping effectively resorts to drinking, the results are often striking. The meek passive person who was careful not to offend anyone, and who would always walk away from any situation that smacked of strife, now roars like a lion and declares that he can beat the hell out of anyone in the room. Indeed, in the privacy of his home and with his wife as a rather safe target, he can become quite abusive and even physically violent. After the effects of alcohol dissipate and the lion reverts back to the lamb, the person cannot believe he said or did all those offensive things.

Anger and resentments cannot be eradicated from life. They can be effectively managed if we don't live in mortal fear of them. There are circumstances when an expression of anger is called for, and when it is quite appropriate to inform someone that the actions are resented.

People who think well of themselves, who have reason to believe they merit friendship, love, and companionship of others, are not apt to be devastated by feelings of hostility. People with positive self-esteem trust their ability to control themselves and are not haunted by fears that feelings will break through into overt deeds. Also, they are aware that although asserting anger may indeed offend someone, it's not the end of the world. They don't feel they must sacrifice everything, including their own dignity, to prevent someone from disliking them. They know that not everyone in the world will like them; if they are liked by only half the world's population, that still gives them some two billion people, and that is sufficient. They approach feelings of hostility with equanimity and without panic.

The same dynamics that are operative in the suppression and repression of anger are often those resulting in pathological passivity. Although self-assertion does not always manifest itself as anger, the person with low self-esteem may perceive any self-assertion as being aggressive.

Case No. 4

Mary is a nun who developed a drinking problem. Mary claimed she was "driven to drink" by the constant anger and frustration resulting from everyone taking advantage of her. Because of her artistic skills, other teachers always asked her to illustrate things for them or design displays for their classes. She felt the principal was exploiting her willingness to help by asking her to take on extra assignments. Mary always complied with these requests, even when she was exhausted and behind in her own work. She was angry at others for being inconsiderate of her. Mary never said "no" to any request made of her. Refusal was simply not in her repertoire. Any request automatically elicited compliance, and this made her so furious that she drank, she said, to get rid of her anger.

Mary's problem with anger and her preference for passivity was present in her youth. Mary's mother was a very domineering person, one not to be disobeyed. Mary recalled how worked up she would become because of her mother's unreasonable demands.

It is of interest that Mary chose to become a nun and adopt a lifestyle that required absolute obedience. Although she had little difficulty in accepting the dictates of her superiors, her resentment of feeling compelled to acquiesce to everyone else's desires got the better of her. Although stress such as this can be handled in other ways, Mary resorted to alcohol every time she became frustrated.

This "I can't say no to anyone" syndrome is encountered in nonalcoholics as well. However, when present in the alcoholic, changing this pattern is an important part of the personality transformation in recovery. Since much of this syndrome, consisting of the extraordinary fear of losing someone's favor, is a reflection of the negative self-image, it follows that growth in self-esteem incident to recovery can bring about the necessary changes.

CHAPTER IX

FEELINGS

"If there is anything common to all alcoholics," one recovering alcoholic said, "it's fear."

There are various types of fear; fear of failure, fear of rejection, fear of isolation, fear of being dominated, fear of abandonment, fear of losing control, even fear of fear.

It is quite obvious that in all types of fear, the fear is of something considered to be overpowering and overwhelming. A person generally doesn't fear something over which he or she feels mastery. Hence, negative self-image and low self-esteem are very much involved in fear, because to the extent that one feels more adequate, competent, and capable, to that extent fear becomes diminished.

One type of fear, which is not often considered, is fear of *feelings*. Now that may sound absurd. Why would one fear feelings? What is there about feelings that could be so threatening? While there may not be satisfactory answers to these questions, I believe the phenomenon is nevertheless a fact. Some people *do* fear feelings, and it seems that in some alcoholics one of the functions of alcohol is to anesthetize feelings, any kind of feelings.

I have encountered some alcoholics in treatment who are at a loss in dealing with feelings. One young man spoke of his marriage and his three children. "I went through the motions of being a husband and father," he said. "I wouldn't know what love was if it were right in front of me." This is particularly true of people who begin using alcohol and/or other drugs early in their lives, and who may have never had exposure to feelings, having spent most of their adolescent and adult lives in a state of emotional anesthesia. The first encounter with feelings—hate, pain, love, guilt, sympathy, grief—may be so frightening that they run back to the chemical anesthetic.

If this appears absurd, it is only because many of us have grown up with feelings; we are familiar with them, and we take them for granted. To someone who has been devoid of feelings, any intense feeling can provoke fear because he or she doesn't know what to do with this feeling. It may be likened to the experience when, after spending long hours in utter darkness, you're suddenly confronted by bright light. The sudden illumination can actually be painful, and you shield your eyes to bring back the more comfortable darkness.

There are probably many circumstances that result in detachment from feelings. One young man in therapy described his childhood wherein the only way he could survive was to stop feeling emotions. The attitude of his family toward him—or at least this was how he perceived it— was so bitter that he defended himself by turning off all feelings. "I built walls around myself. Lots of walls. I wasn't going to let anybody close enough to be able to hurt me." Unfortunately, the walls were barriers not only to pain, but also to love, compassion, and trust.

It is not necessary to have a grossly abnormal childhood in order to be a nonfeeling person. There are many people who appear to be perfectly normal in their behavior, yet are essentially mechanical robots. They may raise their children in an emotionally sterile atmosphere, providing them with all the necessities of life, except for love and warmth. Children from such an environment may have great difficulty dealing with feelings, and one method of managing feelings when they are uncomfortable is to anesthetize one-self to them.

A group of psychologists conducted a study comparing monkeys raised with three different types of mothers.* Group A was reared by normal, monkey mothers. Group B was provided nutrition by milk pumped through breasts of a monkey mannequin, a dummy covered with fur, against which the young could cuddle. Group C monkeys were nurtured by a wire mannequin, which provided adequate milk, but neither warmth nor comfort. Movies showing the behavior of these three groups of monkeys as they grew up are fascinating. Monkeys of Groups A and B behaved quite normally. Monkeys of Group C are frightened and withdrawn. They avoid any new object put into their cage. Rather than explore it as normal monkeys would do, they run into a corner and hide. They are unattracted by monkeys of the opposite sex, and those female monkeys of this group who do become mothers show no sign of maternal caring or affection for their young.

There are some people who may be bright, enterprising, and successful, but aren't able to show any warmth, or for that matter any feeling whatever. They function like computers, with carefully calculated behavior. They don't smile spontaneously, nor do they cry. They don't caress or kiss a child. Even their anger is mechanical, carefully measured, and controlled. To children raised in an environment such as this, feelings may be foreign.

Whereas all feelings come in gradations, from very mild to extremely intense, this may not appear so to the person who has not experienced feelings in the developmental years. To this person, feelings may be an "all or none" phenomenon. Any type of dislike may be equated with hate, which in turn may be seen as identical to a killing

---

* H. F. Harlow, "The Nature of Love," *American Psychologist,* 1958, 13, 673–685.

instinct. Love may be a total self-centered possessiveness. Sexual feelings, because of their inherent intensity, may be overwhelming. This person may perceive having feelings as being completely dominated by instinctual drives over which one has little or no control, and the only way to cope with feelings is not to have them. If and when the person discovers that alcohol is an emotional anesthetic, he or she may find it much simpler to function with feelings that have been anesthetized rather than having to exert constant control over them.

For these people, discontinuing the use of alcohol may bring them face-to-face with their feelings, and this may be distinctly uncomfortable. The reaction may range from mild discomfort to anxiety and panic. Crucial in the treatment of these people is to help them gain enough faith in themselves to be able to trust themselves. They must get to know that they have the ability to control feelings, and that they are not helpless slaves to their instincts. This represents something of a paradox. Actively drinking alcoholics believe they *can* control alcohol which, in fact, they can*not* control. On the other hand, they may believe they have *no* control whatever over their feelings, over which they *can* indeed exert control.

It is most rewarding to observe some alcoholics as they go through their course in a treatment center. A person who is uptight and rigid, walking and moving with the angling character of a toy tin soldier, showing no spontaneous facial expression whatever, gradually becomes a flesh and blood human being. Sometimes near miraculous transformations may be observed, even in as short a period as four weeks.

Case No. 5

Jerry is a young man of 23 who was admitted to a treatment center after eight years of using alcohol, pain pills, sedatives, and amphetamines. On the day following his admission, he encountered me walking down the corridor and asked if he could have a few moments alone with me. He then fell upon my shoulder and began crying bitterly, "I can't take it, Doc! I can't take it! It hurts so bad. I never felt any pain like this before. Help me, Doc! Give me something. I can't take the way I feel."

After Jerry calmed down, I told him about a woman who had suffered severe injuries in an automobile accident, which resulted in many nerves being severed which carry sensations from the upper right arm. Surgeons tried to repair the nerves, but it would be weeks before the outcome of the surgery would be known. During these weeks, the right arm hung down lifeless, like a heavy sack of cement. She was very depressed and discouraged of ever having use of her right arm again.

One day someone dropped a lit cigarette on her right hand, and she felt the pain of the burn. She jumped up and ecstatically screamed, "I can feel! I can feel! It hurts! I can feel!" To anyone else, pain would be unpleasant. To this young woman, pain was a joy because it indicated that her ability to feel was returning.

I told Jerry that since age fifteen he had been living as a zombie, anesthetized with alcohol or other drugs, and unable to feel *any* emotion. True, he had not felt much pain, but he couldn't have experienced any pleasant sensation either. Now that he would be off drugs, he would be able to feel again. The fact that he could feel pain should be an indication that, with the appropriate adjustments in his life, he would be able to feel the joy that he could derive from living.

CHAPTER X

NARCISSISM

A woman came to an alcoholism clinic seeking advice on what to do about her husband. She related the familiar litany of alcoholic behavior. "He is an absolute tyrant," she said. "He terrorizes the whole house. The children live in fear of him. In fact, I hate to admit it, but sometimes he is more tolerable when he's been drinking than when he is dry."

The alcoholic described here is one of the more difficult types, at least as far as the family is concerned. He demands absolute obedience, intimidates everyone with his demands, and has an insatiable need for recognition and admiration. Unfortunately, because his behavior may be so intolerable, he doesn't get the admiration he craves, although he can often exact virtual total submission.

This type of person is generally struggling with such intense feelings of low self-esteem that living would be intolerable unless he or she had something to alleviate these feelings. When intoxicated, the person may be sufficiently anesthetized so that he or she feels nothing. When not anesthetized with alcohol, the person is apt to demand virtual worship by anyone over whom he or she has any control, whether family members or subordinates. Assuming a god-like role gives a fleeting feeling of self-worth. It seems paradoxical, but very often the person who behaves as the "world's greatest," is actually doing so because he or she feels personally bankrupt.

This person is so exquisitely sensitive that almost anything one does can be interpreted as a slight. If the person thinks anyone else was accorded greater recognition, he or she may react violently. If the person is not given what he or she feels to be an appropriate place of honor at a social or community affair, he or she becomes enraged. If the person hears anyone else being praised, he or she is certain to say something to deflate the other person.

People who have good self-esteem do not need to be reminded how good they are. They can afford to be humble and are not easily offended, simply because they are not overly sensitive.

The angry behavior and the unrealistic demands that a person makes generally result in people becoming alienated from him or her. This loss of love, intimacy, and personal support further depresses an already low self-esteem. Inasmuch as this person's mechanism of compensating for low self-esteem is to deflate others and seek praise from those whom he or she can control, both these traits are intensified as the self-esteem progressively drops. A vicious cycle is set in motion, so that his or her demeanor becomes more and more intolerable. At the same time, suffering increases as feelings of self-esteem plummet, and the person is likely to increase drinking both in quantity and frequency to escape the pain. Soon the excessive drinking erodes whatever is left of the person's performance, and as the latter deteriorates, self-esteem is further lowered, resulting in aggravation of both the angry behavior and the drinking.

Although it is often necessary to take a "tough love" approach to the alcoholic, or to "detach with love," this is because protecting the alcoholic from the natural consequences of drinking usually prevents his or her coming to terms with the illness. Let me explain.

Just as there is an immutable law of gravity that states water will flow downhill and never uphill, so there is a law of human gravity which dictates that a person will move from a condition perceived to be one of greater distress to a condition perceived to be one of lesser distress, never in the reverse direction.

Since alcohol is an anesthetic, discontinuing the use of alcohol will result, at least initially, in experiencing some discomfort. According to the principle just stated, a human being is actually incapable of making a choice which would lead to greater distress. Discontinuance of alcohol can occur *if and only if* the alcoholic begins to perceive the drinking as being more distressful than abstinence. This often occurs when the alcoholic reaches "rock bottom." Any manipulations or reactions by significant others in the alcoholic's environment to protect him or her from the natural consequences of drinking are likely to delay the reaching of rock bottom and prolong the drinking.

It is for this reason that people in the alcoholic's environment—spouse, children, parents, relatives, physician, employer, pastor, friends—are cautioned not to be "enablers." They must learn how to detach with love and consideration.*

This is totally different from aggressing against the alcoholic. Degrading, belittling, or shaming the alcoholic in front of others, or doing anything to insult and offend him or her is not "tough love." Such actions will only serve to make the alcoholic feel worse about self, and depressing the already poor self-esteem of the alcoholic generally leads to more intense drinking. The alcoholic who uses alcohol as an anesthetic does so because he or she hurts. It is absurd to believe that further hurt is going to eliminate his or her recourse to the anesthetic.

Furthermore, if the alcoholic recognizes alcohol to be

---

* For more information on detaching with love and consideration, see Abraham Twerski's *Caution: Kindness Can Be Dangerous to the Alcoholic,* Prentice-Hall, Englewood Cliffs, NJ, 1981.

causing the misery, he or she is likely to get rid of the alcohol. If it is a punitive spouse who is making him or her suffer, the alcoholic will get rid of the spouse rather than the alcohol.

The appropriate posture towards the alcoholic is thus a complex one, and one which at first glance might appear to be contradictory. Alcoholics must be allowed to experience the consequences of their drinking and the pain which they are inflicting upon *themselves,* but no one should attempt primarily to hurt the alcoholic in order to curtail the drinking. Quite the contrary, while the "detachment" allows them to experience what alcohol is doing to them, any way in which their self-esteem can be *preserved* will be advantageous to recovery.

CHAPTER XI
PERFECTIONISM

One of the patterns seen in some people with drinking problems is a tendency toward perfectionism. At first glance, this might appear ludicrous. What could be more self-contradictory than a person who is perfectionist drinking alcoholically and thereby grossly diminishing his efficiency and making himself vulnerable to hundreds of errors? This is indeed a very logical observation, but when we remember that in the process of denial and with the peculiar kind of logic characteristic of the alcoholic many gross contradictions occur, this phenomenon is not too surprising after all.

Perfectionism may be one of the mechanisms employed by a person with a low self-esteem and deep feelings of insecurity. No one enjoys making a mistake, but to the person with low self-esteem making an error can be devastating. Feelings of inadequacy may drive the person to demonstrate to self and others that he or she is not awkward or incompetent. Making a mistake would just confirm that opinion, and this must be avoided at all costs. The person may therefore become scrupulous in everything, spending a great deal of time on minute details, rechecking everything numerous times. Even after all the effort, the person still lives in fear of having made a mistake.

The irony is that all the time and effort consumed in

trying to avoid mistakes can be so draining and exhausting that the person cannot properly accomplish whatever is supposed to be done, and thus by trying to avoid trivial mistakes ends up making big ones. When major errors are discovered, the person becomes even more upset and tries to avoid any mistake by intensifying obsessive behavior. This leads into a vicious cycle of anxiety, tension, and dissatisfaction.

If this person finds relief from the discomfort in drinking, everything is apt to be aggravated many times over. Since alcohol is a central nervous system depressant, it causes an actual decrease in efficiency and deterioration in performance. But this deterioration is apt to intensify the defensive obsession of getting everything done just right, and so the use of alcohol causes more turns of the vicious cycle. At the same time, alcohol can so distort the drinker's thinking that at times even the most fouled up situations appear just fine. During moments of clarity, the person may realize how horribly messed up everything is, and of course, is then very likely to resort to alcohol to escape this painful awareness.

When recovery begins and the alcoholic no longer lives in the oblivion of a mind clouded with alcohol, the reality of the situation must be faced, even though sometimes all there is to see is a heap of ruins. This is difficult for anyone to take, but to the perfectionist it is virtually intolerable, and avoiding return to alcohol requires a great deal of effort and support.

As abstinence from alcohol persists and the alcoholic begins to function without the disabling influence of alcohol, the perfectionistic traits are still likely to remain. These have been part of the personality for years and they don't just disappear when the drinking stops. If anything, the realization of how bad things have become further depresses low self-esteem and can intensify perfectionistic drives, possibly causing the person to become perfectionistic in recovery.

Perfection is simply not real. It's just not within the range of human achievement. Since only God is perfect, the quest for perfection may be part of the alcoholic's delusion that he or she is God-like, with the feeling of omnipotence that this entails. As long as a person sees self in this way there can be no surrender to, or acceptance of, a Higher Power.

We can now appreciate the full value of the philosophy of Alcoholics Anonymous as expressed in the following paragraph:

"No one among us has been able to maintain anything like perfect adherence to these principles. We are not saints. The point is, that we are willing to grow along spiritual lines. The principles we have set down are guides to progress. We claim spiritual progress rather than spiritual perfection."*

Case No. 6

Evaline is a young attorney, very intelligent and capable, who began her recovery in an alcoholism treatment center, and whose first four months in recovery were very smooth; too smooth in fact. One day she called her counselor, confessing that she had just had a two day "slip." She was devastated. The counselor told Evaline that many people, especially early in recovery, have a recurrence of the delusion of "control," and need to find out the hard way that powerlessness over alcohol is in fact true. He urged her to increase her attendance at meetings. "Have you told your sponsor?" he asked. "Oh, don't make me do that," Evaline pleaded. "I can't tell her. She thinks I'm perfect."

In the conversation that followed, the counselor was able to point out to Evaline that she had not yet overcome her perfectionism, and that by not telling her sponsor about

---

* *Alcoholics Anonymous,* published by A. A. World Services, Inc., New York, NY, p. 60.

her relapse, she was not only being dishonest, but was also allowing the need to present herself as perfect to undo her recovery program. He read her the paragraph of the Big Book cited earlier. "Don't try to be perfect," he said. "That is completely unattainable, and you'll be doomed to frustration. Furthermore, if you somehow succeed in being perfect, you'll make all of us avoid you because we can't stand perfect people. We like people who are human just like the rest of us. We try to progress, and we try to improve ourselves. It's terribly uncomfortable to be in the company of somebody who is perfect."

Evaline said she didn't know how something like that could have happened to her. Her four months of sobriety had gone along perfectly, without a hitch. She had never even once craved a drink. The counselor responded that having four smooth months is probably the worst curse a person early in recovery can have. This allowed Evaline's defenses to fall and her delusions of perfection to re-emerge. As unfortunate as her slip was, this is what she needed to bring her back to the reality that she is a human being after all. She is a very fine human being, but one with human limitations, and one who needs to realize that only one Being is perfect. Evaline is now discovering what true self-esteem is. It consists of appreciating oneself for what one is and what one has the potential to become, and not some grandiose fantasy.

CHAPTER XII

SELF-ESTEEM IN WOMEN

The problem of self-esteem becomes more complex and intensified in the woman alcoholic. Everything that has been said earlier about self-esteem prior to the onset of alcoholic drinking applies to the woman as well, but there can be both quantitative and qualitative changes in the woman. After the onset of drinking, the impact on self-esteem in the woman is often much more devastating than in the male alcoholic, and recovery may be more difficult.

Feminists have pointed out that first grade primers have defined stereotyped male roles for Dick and female roles for Jane. They also observe that little boys have doctor kits, which invariably have a picture of a male child with a stethoscope, while the nurses' kits show a little girl with a nurse's cap, and are assumed to be girls' toys.

There is a profound distinction that is even more fundamental than career roles or businessman versus housewife, which is impressed on children even in the pre-verbal stage, when they are lulled to sleep with nursery rhymes. Many Mother Goose collections declare:

What are little boys made of?
What are little boys made of?
Frogs and snails and puppy dog tails
That's what little boys are made of.
What are little girls made of?

What are little girls made of?
Sugar and spice and everything nice
That's what little girls are made of.

It is thus conveyed to the child that males are biologically composed of some rather rough ingredients. Should a male manifest aggression, vulgarity, dishonesty, or other base traits, he is pretty much in character with his constitutional makeup. Neither he nor anyone else should rightfully expect much else from him. Not so for the female, who is composed of dainty and noble ingredients. Anything that looks, tastes, or acts other than one would expect from "sugar and spice and everything nice" is a gross perversion of her fundamental substance.

Implied in this fundamental difference in composition is that men who do no evil are saints, since obviously they have managed to overcome their natural evil inclinations. Should they act in keeping with their assumed biology, they are hardly to be condemned. They are punished only when they have allowed their natural drives to be grossly injurious to others.

Women, on the other hand, are hardly to be commended for being decent, for this is their natural state. The slightest manifestation of anything that is not of the highest virtue is criticized. The expectation of many women, by others and by themselves, is that they should be innocent, pure, and self-sacrificing.

If, as we may assume, this biologic assertion is scientifically incorrect, girls are in for some difficulty. If feminine protoplasm, like the masculine kind, really lusts and hates and craves and envies, and has all the characteristics of protoplasm, then the woman who believes that all these feelings should be alien to her is apt to be very critical of herself, condemning herself for what she perceives as a perversion of her true nature. She is apt to feel very alone, since she may assume that all other women are probably truer to their noble ingredients, and that she is unique in possessing these despicable and unladylike traits.

All the classic defense mechanisms—unconscious repression, conscious suppression, overcompensation, projection, disassociation—are brought into play to conceal from others the horrible "truth" about herself. Certainly others should not be allowed to come too close, lest they discover the truth. Withdrawal, alienation, and fear of intimacy are all characteristics of the woman who tries to keep her terrible secret from being discovered; and often these are the characteristics of many a woman who develops a drinking problem.

These women who develop difficulties resulting in an alcohol problem, often do so in response to the double standard conflict. There may be a variety of responses, but at the risk of oversimplification, they can be divided into two groups.

The first is the young woman who, often in adolescence, decides that this "sugar and spice" business is absurd, and that she, too, is made of some rather base ingredients. She may react in the manner she thinks appropriate to her newly discovered identity. She may reject all social values with total defiance of authority, and become the runaway, the tramp, sexually promiscuous, and may indulge heavily in alcohol and/or other drugs.

The second and much more frequent response has been to adopt the socially expected role as the ideal wife and mother, often with a traditional female job as secretary, teacher, or nurse. If there are elements of self-assertion and aggressiveness, these are generally repressed. The compensation for sacrificing these drives is the love and support of a devoted husband and children, and the approval of society. Drinking may not be of any significance as long as things go well.

If, however, the delicate balance is offset by loss of these compensatory factors, especially by divorce, loss of income, death of a close family member, children leaving the home, or by seeing close friends successfully adopt lifestyles which fulfill their self-assertive drives, this woman may become very unhappy and dissatisfied. This depression may take her to a psychiatrist or family physician. She may find relief with tranquilizers, or discover the tranquilizing effect of alcohol, and then develop dependency on these substances.

Changes in the lifestyles of women, with greater penetration into the marketplace, may have considerable emotional cost. The competitiveness of the business world, the need to sometimes push others aside and get there first, are not the natural outgrowths of a child cultivated out of sugar and spice. Adaptation to this new setting may generate considerable stress, and may result in an intrapsychic conflict, where the successful woman and the "good girl" can't co-exist in the same person. With so many business activities centering around drinking, there is increasing exposure and pressure to drink. Furthermore, the woman who feels that equality with males in the business world requires adoption of male behavior, may feel the need to keep up with the alcohol consumption of her male counterparts.

The effects of alcohol on the woman are again subject to double standard judgment. When a male loses his inhibitions he is often thought of as more manly, whereas for the woman it is most unladylike to let loose her inhibitions. There is widespread belief that a woman who drinks excessively must be promiscuous. The drinking mother is considered irresponsible and negligent, derelict in her parental duties. This judgment is not as likely to be made of the drinking father.

Although alcoholism as a disease has been well established, it has not yet been universally accepted. Centuries of thinking alcoholism caused debauchery and moral degeneracy won't change completely in several decades. But even where the disease of alcoholism has been accepted, this enlightenment is also subject to the double standard. Only very recently has it been recognized that the bulk of data on alcoholism has been accumulated in studies of male alcoholics, and that these findings can't be assumed to be valid for women. The impact of this assumption on treatment can be far-reaching, because applying principles of male needs to women can be most misleading.

There has also been an increasing realization that alcoholism is a family disease. Although this means different things to different people, there is nevertheless some awareness that optimal therapy requires some involvement of the family in the treatment process. Yet, although Alcoholics Anonymous is not completely male-populated, the composition of Al-Anon is still disproportionately female. It seems the wife is more apt to accept she has a role in her husband's disease and recovery, and is more willing to look at herself and how her own personality traits may have dovetailed with those of her alcoholic husband. The absence of males at Al-Anon may mean that men have greater difficulty in accepting any part whatever in their wives' condition. It is more often seen as "her thing," and it is her responsibility to set things right. There's simply no need for "me to look at myself" in regard to her alcoholism.

Along the same line, it has been demonstrated that a wife will generally continue the marriage with an alcoholic husband much more frequently than a husband will with an alcoholic wife. Again the double standard.

The denial of alcoholism which is so characteristic of this condition, and which precludes the alcoholic's seeking help, is very often intensified in the woman. Whereas the "tough love" attitude adopted by the significant others can foster an earlier and less devastating "rock bottom," the greater likelihood of a cover-up when the alcoholic is a woman delays acceptance of help.

Thus the low self-esteem, which is apt to be more profound in the pre-alcoholic woman and which may contribute to the development of alcoholism, and the intensification of negative self-feelings which is apt to be very severe in the woman, combine to make the condition more complex and more resistive to treatment. Once in treatment, the lack of sensitivity to a woman's needs may still be encountered in some largely male-oriented treatment programs and may render treatment less effective.

CHAPTER XIII
ALCOHOLISM AS A DISEASE

One of the worst obstacles to the alcoholic's recovery may be the drinker's belief that alcoholism is a failure of the will, and in order to gain control over alcohol the drinker must properly exert willpower. This misconception results in hundreds of futile attempts at controlling one's drinking. Promises are made to self and others, and when the drinker succeeds in abstaining for several weeks or months, he or she is even more convinced that it is merely a matter of asserting one's will. It is only after repeated failures and with cumulative effects of these failures constituting a "rock bottom" that the drinker comes to the realization that alcoholic drinking or alcoholism is not contingent upon willpower.

In some alcoholics there is a physiologic abnormality in the way the body handles alcohol. Perhaps this is an inherited metabolic abnormality or something which develops after long periods of drinking or even a combination of these two factors. It has long been evident that alcohol affects the alcoholic in a different manner than it does the nonalcoholic. Personality changes that occur in some alcoholics do not occur in nonalcoholics. Loss of control that is characteristic of many alcoholics after the first drink is not present in the nonalcoholic. The compulsive drive for alcohol does not occur in the nonalcoholic. On the other hand, for the nonalcoholic, alcohol doesn't do what it does for many alcoholics; namely, change their perception of themselves and reality as a whole.

It is these and other different phenomena of alcohol in the alcoholic that comprise the disease concept of alcoholism. There is something fundamentally different about the body's handling of alcohol, and the alcoholic is no more at fault for having this abnormality than is the diabetic for having that particular metabolic abnormality.

Our culture is one where drinking is not only socially condoned, but actively encouraged. Virtually all social events feature alcohol quite prominently; toasting is done with a drink, and the media constantly depict the virtues of drinking. Even religious rites include alcohol, and the scriptures are filled with the virtues of wine.

One of the disease phenomena of alcohol is that alcohol actually prevents alcoholics from knowing they are being adversely affected. In other words, denial is part of the disease itself, rather than just a response to the condition. The alcoholic must therefore often wait for the harmful consequences of drinking to occur before denial can be overcome.

As long as the drinker considers alcoholism to be an inadequate self-assertion or a failure to exercise one's will, he or she condemns self for drinking and the resulting consequences. Defensively, the drinker may project the blame onto others, but fundamentally blames himself. This self-disapproval intensifies the pre-existing feelings of inadequacy and low self-esteem.

Realizing alcoholism is a disease for which no one is to blame, including the drinker, lifts the burden off the shoulders of the alcoholic. He or she no longer needs punishment for being unable to control alcohol. Inability to control does not indicate a weak personality or a degenerate, any more than a penicillin allergy reflects on the personality of the allergic individual. The alcoholic must avoid alcohol just as the allergic person must avoid penicillin. Acceptance of the disease eliminates a troublesome source of depressed self-esteem, and paves the way for acceptance of effective treatment.

CHAPTER XIV

TOWARD POSITIVE SELF-ESTEEM

How is a distorted self-concept overcome? If self-esteem is contingent upon a true self-awareness, just how can awareness be achieved?

Nothing positive can be accomplished as long as the brain is under the influence of alcohol or other drugs. Therapists who try to work with an alcoholic patient without insisting on total abstinence from mind-altering substances will generally find their efforts futile.

Even with a clear mind, one usually can't correct a faulty self-perception without some external help. This is because sensually derived information is much more impressive to a person than that derived from analysis or contemplation. If a person has auditory or visual hallucinations, you can present him with a logical and convincing argument why he can't possibly be seeing or hearing something that doesn't exist in reality, but all your efforts will be in vain. When he has a sense that he sees or hears something, there is no logical way of convincing him that he doesn't see or hear what he *is* seeing or hearing.

Think of a person who looks at the world through colored lenses. He sees everything tinted, not because things are really so, but because a colored lens is distorting true perception. The individual who has somehow developed a distorted self-concept is looking at himself through a kind of psychological lens that distorts his view. The difference is that the person wearing the colored glasses knows there is something altering his perception and can easily remove the glasses to achieve a true picture. But the person with a distorted self-concept doesn't know perception is distorted. He has no glasses before his eyes. The "psychological lenses" are inside his mind somewhere and can't easily be removed. Furthermore, he has no awareness that there is any distortion. To the contrary, he is absolutely certain that what he sees in himself is reality. Arguing with him that what he sees is not reality is generally futile.

Since the person's self-perception is distorted, his self-concept may begin to change only if he can accept that others perceive him as good and worthy. However, this may be difficult to communicate to him, since our culture is one where social graces dictate that everyone generally says nice things to one another. There is no reason to assume that a positive statement made by another person is his true opinion rather than the usual meaningless and socially expected compliment.

In the days when I served as Rabbi, my wife and I were invited for dinner by a young couple whose marriage ceremony I had performed several months earlier. Unfortunately for us, the newlywed housewife fancied herself to be a gourmet cook. Her concept of gourmet was any exotic and unusual dish, and she prepared seven courses of *very* unusual dishes. I became quite nauseated after the first course, and the nausea only increased in intensity with every course served. Yet, because I was my host's guest, I could give no indication of my revulsion. Never in my life had I prayed so intensely, and the host of heaven was undoubtedly taken aback by this strange prayer, "Dear God, all I ask of You is to let me live long enough to vomit."

When we stood at the door and said our good-byes to our hosts, the only thought occupying my mind was, "Soon I will be in the privacy of my bathroom and I will be able to throw up." I nevertheless said what has to be the greatest lie ever told since creation, "Thank you for a wonderful evening. The dinner was lovely, and I enjoyed it immensely."

When social finesse dictates that we lie, how can anyone give credence to any favorable observation someone communicates to him?

Was I really kind to this young woman? I don't think so. I never visited their home again, and I'm certain the next couple she invited to dinner were served the same revulsive concoctions we had been served, for didn't I assure her how delightful they were? And if that couple lied as I did, and like I, never set foot in their home again, the pattern must have repeated itself until for all I know, this young woman has no friends left in the world.

Had I been truly kind and considerate, I would have said, "Please, don't go to such a fuss! People who wish to spend an evening with you are not starved for food, but are there to enjoy your company. Next time, just heat up some frozen dinners."

The empty compliments we generally give to one another are without impact. Verbal statements will do little or nothing to alter another's distorted self-concept. If our communications are to be of value, they must be genuine and convey a free flow of feeling which accompanies whatever we say.

I have seen this occur numerous times in an alcoholism rehabilitation center. Here the patient associates with staff members who try to be honest and truthful. The therapist is geared to say only what he or she feels, whether this be complimentary or critical. The therapist's observation may be correct or incorrect, but it's not a lie insofar as personal impressions are concerned. The staff is trained not to withhold feelings, and to voice their innermost impressions. Among the staff and the resident population a setting of honesty and straightforwardness develops. The patient then believes when a positive appraisal is made, it is valid, because when the appraisal is negative, it's not withheld.

The support of staff and peers in the rehabilitation center can provide the alcoholic with courage to take an honest look at self. This process is continued in the A.A. fellowship with the help of a sponsor and the companionship of fellow recovering alcoholics who know their greatest kindness to one another is to be as frank and truthful as they can manage to be. It's then that the observation of others can be given some credibility.

Prior to the advent of residential treatment centers, the whole process was generally initiated within the A.A. fellowship. The residential treatment center can provide a significant headstart by having the alcoholic undergo a rather intensive beginning and self-knowledge in a structured environment, free of the risk of relapse.

The ideal of anything hardly exists anywhere. It would be foolish to say that everyone involved in A.A. is the perfect example of honesty, and that the fellowship is without pretension. But it can be said that within the fellowship a recovering alcoholic can find the sincerity, support, and direction that will allow for better self-awareness.

CHAPTER XV

SELF-ESTEEM AND SURRENDER

Alcoholics Anonymous works in many ways, and does different things for different people at different times. A.A. contributes toward the development of positive self-esteem, and has achieved the most durable and widespread recoveries.

The first and most vital step in recovery is that of *surrender:* the acceptance that a person has lost control of drinking and that life has become unmanageable. Many people perceive loss of control as a limitation or weakness. It is difficult to accept what is perceived as a weakness when the person feels very inadequate. For the person with low self-esteem, admission of a weakness is threatening. The lower one's self-esteem, the more threatening is the realization of loss of control. The delusion of having control over alcohol when it is evident to everyone else that there is no control, is particularly tenacious in the advanced stages of alcoholism.

I've often heard actively drinking alcoholics say, "A.A. isn't for me because I'm an agnostic; I don't believe in God." This generally isn't true. It's not that alcoholics don't believe in God, but rather that they believe themselves to be God, at least their own God. Their psychological systems have defended against feelings of low self-esteem by developing delusions of grandiosity. "I don't need any help. I don't have an alcohol problem. I can stop any time I want to."

Such blatant contradictions of reality can come only from delusions of omnipotence.

There can be no acceptance of a Higher Power as long as one considers self the highest power in one's life. To the agnostic who objects to involvement in A.A. because it is God oriented, I say, "You're jumping ahead of yourself. Acceptance of a Higher Power doesn't come until the second step. Let's start with the first step." Once the person accepts a loss of control of drinking, that his or her life has become unmanageable, and that self is not one's highest power, it is a small task to go on to acknowledge that out there somewhere there is a Higher Power.

True surrender cannot occur until there is sufficient positive self-esteem so that accepting loss of control is no longer a serious threat to one's ego. The novice in recovery is probably incapable of true surrender. During the initial phase of recovery, the acceptance of loss of control is invariably compliance rather than surrender.

Things begin to happen early in recovery that pave the way for surrender to occur. As abstinence persists, the person begins to experience an exhilarating feeling. The more than fourteen billion brain cells begin to function together, unimpeded by alcohol. The keenness of thinking increases and one remembers clearly what happened yesterday and the day before. One meets people with many years of sobriety and realizes it's possible to survive and flourish without alcohol. A sense of optimism begins to replace the feeling of despair. Being accepted by countless others in the fellowship, and the realization that one has been a victim of the disease all these years and not a weak-willed moral degenerate, combine to lift one out of depression. Finally, as abstinence continues for a longer period than one can recall in recent years, there comes a sense of pride in being on the winning side of a very tough battle.

These initial positive sensations give one a beginning

sense of self-esteem so that getting rid of the omnipotence delusion is no longer so threatening. As sobriety progresses, this self-esteem increases; and as one's sense of self-esteem increases, the threat of admitting loss of control in one aspect of life becomes less dreadful. At this point, true surrender can begin.

As we shall see, the A.A. program is an excellent and perhaps unsurpassed vehicle for development of self-esteem. As one continues to grow in sobriety and feels progressively better about one's self, the acceptance of a limitation becomes even less threatening, and the sense of surrender can become more profound. Surrender is therefore not a one-time event, nor should it remain stagnant. Surrender must grow with one's personality growth. The First Step must be taken over and over again in the course of sobriety. If a person who has been sober in A.A. for fifteen years doesn't have a more profound sense of surrender than the year before, it's because he or she has remained stagnant and hasn't had any personality growth for a year.

Many things contribute to a sense of self-esteem. Realization of the twelve promises or rewards of A.A. converts one's life from a negative vicious cycle to a self-reinforcing growth pattern. Emergence from the state of low self-esteem is absolutely essential for the A.A. program to be optimally effective, since without surrender all else is ineffective. Yet, it is possible for a person to abstain from drinking and have a semblance of sobriety without true surrender. This is a highly dangerous state, filled with risk of relapse.

Elaine is a patient of mine whose recovery is a source of great pride and gratification for me. She is an executive's wife, a woman in her mid-fifties whose life had become totally unmanageable due to alcohol. I guided Elaine through a rehabilitation program, and urged her into A.A.

Elaine had been sober and active in the program for about two years when I happened to meet her sponsor, and I remarked how beautifully she was doing. I was surprised at the sponsor's rather deflating comment, "Yeah, I guess she's doing OK."

"What do you mean, 'doing OK'?" I asked. "Elaine is beautiful! She's marvelous!"

The sponsor shook his head. "Nope, Doc," he said. "Something's wrong with Elaine, and I can't figure it out. She's doing everything by the book, all right. She's chairing, leading, and attending regularly. But there's something wrong there, and I don't know what it is." He shrugged his shoulders, and so did I.

About two months later, Elaine called me to discuss something or other, and after a few minutes on the phone, she apologized with, "Oh, I'm sorry I'm keeping you so long. You have more important things to do."

"Like what?" I asked.

"Well, you have to take care of your patients," she said.

"Sure, I have to take care of my patients," I agreed. "All I'll be doing is talking to them, and now I'm talking to you. Are you telling me it's more important that I talk to someone else rather than to you?"

"Well, you know what I mean," she said.

"No, I don't," I replied. "Not unless you tell me."

"Well, I think it's wonderful that you take time out for people like us," she said.

"People like whom?" I asked.

"You know what I mean," she said.

"Cut out that mind-reading stuff," I answered. "I know only what you tell me."

"Well, I think it's great that you've taken time out for us dregs of humanity," she said.

At this point, I became aware of what Elaine's sponsor had sensed a while back. Elaine was doing everything by the book, but she hadn't made peace with the fact that she was an alcoholic. She couldn't accept this as long as she believed an alcoholic was a third-rate citizen, or as she put it, a dreg of humanity.

It was evident that, although Elaine would get up and say, "My name is Elaine, and I'm an alcoholic," these were only words to her. She programmed her brain to think of herself intellectually as an alcoholic; but at the gut level, where it really counts, she didn't feel she was an alcoholic. She never relinquished the misconception that an alcoholic was not good.

This misconception is one of the causes for a phenomenon we see in the program: people who are dry but not really sober. This may also be one of the main reasons that some people slip after being in the program for several years. If we want to be technical about it, we might say no one ever really loses sobriety. The person who relapses after several years in the program may have been abstinent from alcohol, but may never have attained sobriety. Like Elaine, this person may have mouthed, "I am an alcoholic," from her head, but not out of her heart.

The analysis is rather simple, and all comes down to the First Step of surrender. As long as people feel there is something fundamentally bad about themselves, they can't afford to surrender. They can't admit powerlessness, because their fragile egos will not allow it. Just as the small child boasts of powers ("Look, Ma, no hands") and tends to demonstrate independence simply because of his or her small stature, so the adult who feels small can't yield the feeling of omnipotence and admit powerlessness. When we feel okay about ourselves as *persons,* it's then and only then that we can accept our dependence on others and on a Higher Power. It's only then that we can surrender and take that all-important First Step, without which all the rest are meaningless.

I don't believe successful Twelfth Step work can be done by anyone who, regardless of the length of abstinence, still has the hang-up of feeling like a bad person because he or she is an alcoholic. Our feelings have a way of communicating themselves to others regardless of the words we use. In encountering people in need of help with drinking problems, you can't successfully deliver the message if you believe being alcoholic is not good, because you're conveying this as an assessment of the other people as well. When the unspoken message is, "I consider myself to be less than the best type of person because I'm an alcoholic," the people who receive this message will understand that this is the way they must feel about themselves.

There are many who, like Elaine, get all mixed up between "drinking is bad" and "being an alcoholic is bad." Much of the work that goes on in the initial phase of entering the program must consist of disentangling these two ideas; the newcomer needs to get the feeling that he or she is a fine person, and that an inability to handle alcohol shouldn't lower self-esteem any more than would the inability to take penicillin or eat strawberries because of an allergy.

I think the surrender occurring early in the program is most often an intellectual surrender, and perhaps that is all that can occur initially. But if surrender stops there, little will have been accomplished in the way of personality growth. No one else can successfully look into our hearts and tell us whether we have progressed beyond an intellectual surrender. When we can honestly feel the same about being alcoholic as we would about being allergic to any particular food, for example, and when we feel no less proud of ourselves as persons because of the existence of an alcoholism problem, then we will have arrived.

Incidentally, Elaine, like many others, has made that transition. She is a beautiful person; she is an alcoholic, and now she knows both of these descriptions can be true at the same time.

CHAPTER XVI
SELF-EXAMINATION

To know oneself requires self-examination, a process required by the fourth of the Twelve Steps in A.A.: a searching and fearless moral inventory. This self-scrutiny is of immense help in overcoming a distorted self-concept. However, unless properly done, an inventory can go awry.

Some people are under the impression that an inventory only consists of digging out every misdeed a person has ever done, particularly those consequent to the alcoholism. If one were to stop here, the result could be a massive depression.

Suppose I ask you to do an inventory of my home, and you submit a report that my home is nothing but a garbage dump. I then demand to know how you came to so erroneous a conclusion, and you tell me that you examined my basement and found it full of worthless junk. I admit this is true. I'm a procrastinator, and have repeatedly postponed a much-needed cleaning of the basement, so that a great deal of junk has accumulated there. However, I ask you, why didn't you look at the first floor, where I have a nicely furnished living room, a rather handsome dining room, and a well-equipped kitchen? Why didn't you go up to the second floor, where the bedrooms are nicely furnished, and where my study contains an impressive library? How do you render an inventory after concentrating only on where the garbage accumulated, without looking at the fine and valuable items in the house?

Just as inspecting only the basement doesn't provide a fair evaluation of a house, so does unearthing every negative deed not provide a true personal inventory. The inventory must include all one's positive deeds and qualities as well.

I therefore suggest an inventory be done on a sheet with two columns labeled POSITIVES and NEGATIVES. In the first column should be listed all one's admirable traits and deeds; and in the second column, all those considered uncommendable or reprehensible. If the list in the negative column is long and that in the positive column is sparse, this should immediately alert one to the probable presence of a distorted perception. Even the worst offenders should be able to find some good things they have done in their lifetime. Help should be sought to discover more of the commendable features of one's life and personality.

Let us now look at the negative list. As we analyze these items, we will find many things we regret doing, and recognize their wrongness. If we had the opportunity, we certainly wouldn't repeat them, and we'd act differently now. If this is so, then these were unfortunate mistakes, but ones from which we have learned something. But an experience which serves as a lesson for correcting one's behavior is no longer a negative experience. The valuable lesson gained from these converts them into positive experiences. These should therefore all be crossed out of the negative column and entered into the positive column.

We will list some items negatively because they ended up with bad results. That is, there are things we do with good intentions and that are based upon the best knowledge available to us at the time, but which turn out to have undesirable consequences. But it is a mistake to judge things by how they turn out. No one has the power of prophetic foresight. Actions must be judged to be morally good or bad according to what deliberations and considerations went into the action, and not by the consequences.

We are unfortunately so immersed in economics, that we may not recognize how often we misapply economic standards to moral issues. Economic values may justifiably be based on success and failure. If a person recklessly invests in a stock or business which to everyone's surprise turns out to be highly profitable, that will generally be considered a good decision. If, on the other hand, one seeks competent counsel and studies all issues carefully, and then makes a thought-out investment which turns out to be a disaster, this will invariably be considered by everyone to have been a bad decision. The laws of the marketplace may justify evaluation by outcome. Moral deeds shouldn't be judged in this manner. Undesirable results may indeed flow from good decisions.

Check the negative list for things you did with good intentions, but which you consider to be negative because they had bad results. Cross these out. These can now be seen to belong on the positive side.

By this time the negative column should be rather sparse and the positive column quite full. However, since there is a possibility that one's autobiography may be incomplete and that the interpretation of one's actions may be inaccurate, it is necessary to review one's history with an impartial observer; someone who is patient enough to listen and competent to understand and help, both to recall and analyze one's deeds.

The sense of well-being that one can derive from a thorough and comprehensive personal inventory and from sharing one's history with another person can be most edifying. A thorough and sincere revelation requires courage, and one justifiably feels a better person upon completing a courageous act. There is a distinct sense of relief in unburdening oneself of a great deal of trash that has accumulated over the years. The person comes face-to-face with humanity, and is able to recognize the frailties that make a person human, the strengths that make a potentially great human, and the capabilities to use these strengths to become a master over the frailties, which makes the person a crown jewel of creation.

CHAPTER XVII

DEALING WITH GUILT

Guilt is one of the most potent depressants of self-esteem. This is hardly surprising, since the two can be seen as polar opposites. Guilt is a consequence of feeling that one has done wrong, and self-esteem is generally thought of as relating to feeling that one has done right.

Although guilt is often considered destructive, this is clearly not so. The emotional pain of guilt is comparable to the physical pain sustained in fire. If we didn't feel pain when our hands were in a flame, we would sustain severe burns without being aware of it. Indeed, this is what happens in those diseases where parts of the body lose pain sensation. The person may sustain serious injury, since he or she lacks the pain sensation which would warn of something harmful happening to the body. Guilt is the emotional pain resulting from the realization that one has done something wrong, and as such, it is a healthy feeling when it deters us from doing wrong. The conviction that something is morally wrong would often not suffice to deter someone from committing an act, were it not for the knowledge that one would suffer guilt as a consequence. There is a type of guilt, however, which is abnormal and doesn't serve a constructive purpose. This occurs when a person feels guilty although he or she hasn't done anything that would warrant this feeling.

It is important to understand that pure emotions, in and of themselves, are neither good nor bad. Actions can be judged to be good or bad, but pure feelings are neither.

Suppose someone steps on my toe and I feel pain. The feeling of pain is neither morally good nor morally bad, it's just there. It results when the body tissues are irritated in such a way that the nerve endings convey pain to the brain. How can this feeling be considered to be either good or bad?

So far, so good. Now, when my toe is stepped on and I hurt, there is an automatic, spontaneous, and immediate feeling of resentment and hostility toward whoever inflicted that pain on me. I really have no choice whether or not to feel that hostility and resentment, any more than I have a choice as to whether to feel the pain. I do have a choice as to whether I will remain silent, or say, "Can't you watch where you're going, you clumsy oaf!" or give the person a harsh shove. I have a choice of what action to take, if any, but I don't have a choice of feeling the pain or the hostility. If I have no choice over a feeling, it's meaningless to talk of it as being either good or bad from a moral aspect. It's just there.

There are many feelings over which one has no control. Love, hate, lust, envy, anger, shame, pride—all these can arise spontaneously, without the person willing them into existence. We have a great deal of choice in reacting to any of these feelings, and our actions are appropriately judged as being morally good or bad; but to talk about the morality of pure feelings is almost meaningless; almost, because there's one reservation which we will soon discuss.

Psychologists have pointed out that sometimes our conscience may not make this distinction between feeling and behavior, and will treat a thought as though it were an act. Thus, a person's conscience may torment one's self for having *felt* hatred just as if one had injured or killed the hated person. The conscience may punish one for desiring someone else's spouse, just as if the act of adultery had been committed, and for envying another person just as though someone had actually stolen his or her belongings.

Guilt because of feelings over which a person has no control is not healthy guilt. It doesn't lend itself to amends and often requires some type of therapy for its disappearance.

Occasionally a therapist confuses these issues, and believes *all* guilt is pathologic, and that a psychologically healthy person should never feel guilt of any type. This is patently false.

The Eighth and Ninth Steps in A.A. deal with realistic guilt. If you've harmed or offended anyone, do whatever you can to set things right. You may need to apologize or perhaps make restitution. Make every effort to correct those wrongs which existed *in reality* and which lend themselves to correction. These are not to be analyzed away in therapy, because they are real phenomena rather than sick symptoms.

However, as far as feelings are concerned, we can't do anything about having them, and as the serenity prayer dictates, things we can't do anything about have to be accepted. We must accept these feelings as part of our humanity.

But A.A. doesn't stop here. The Sixth Step states that although we cannot remove any traits which are an integral part of our being, God can, and will do so if asked and when, in His infinite wisdom, He knows this should be done.

We can't expect God or a Higher Power to remove undesirable traits until we have first done everything in our power to eliminate them. The person who doesn't restrain hostile behavior and expects God to remove all feelings of hostility will not find any prayers answered because the person has failed to do his or her own share of the job first. The person who is bothered by erotic impulses and asks God to remove them but continues to indulge in provocative and stimulating literature can hardly expect Divine intervention. Only when we've done all that is within our power can we ask God to take over.

Our self-esteem is greatly improved when guilt is dealt with appropriately. Making amends produces both humility and a feeling of healthy righteousness. Understanding our humanity, getting help with pathologic feelings, and asking the help of a Higher Power for that which is beyond our power, contributes to a sense of positive self-worth. The devastating effects of guilt on self-esteem can thus be overcome.

CHAPTER XVIII

GROWTH

Even when alcoholics recover and overcome their low self-esteem problem, a trace of the negative self-image remains, and can be resurrected by various challenges. It's much like a folded page; when straightened, a crease remains which is likely to result in the page folding again upon the slightest pressure.

Frances, the physician in Chapter VIII, began doing very well in her recovery. She achieved good sobriety, and a fairly responsible position in a health facility.

After several months on the job, Frances called her therapist, complaining of very deep depression. "I just can't make it," she said. "Everything is too much for me." The therapist listened attentively and reassured her that she was, in fact, able to perform well, and encouraged her to continue.

Several months later, Frances called again. "This time it's really bad," she said. She had overcome the previous depressive episode which had been relatively brief. She then related some personal problems she was now having since her divorce and since assuming sole responsibility for the children, financially as well as emotionally.

Every few months, there was a similar call. Each time, the report was that the previous problem had been resolved, but this time things were different and *really* bad. Finally the therapist called Frances in for a conference.

The therapist pointed out to Frances that each of her calls in which she complained of incapacitating depression had coincided with some new challenge that was confronting her. As a result of her functioning adequately at a particular level for a period of time, she was faced with some new demands. Any new demands reawakened her old feelings of insecurity, inadequacy, and fear of failure, resulting in a crisis in which she felt overwhelmed and depressed.

The therapist pointed out to Frances that at each crisis point she had two choices: escape into drinking or master the challenge.

Mastery of a challenge is always a growth experience which elevates the person to a higher level of functioning. As Frances progressed to this higher level, additional demands were made either by herself or others, and again a crisis occurred. He showed her that the crises were the natural consequences of satisfactory functioning, because successful performance at one level for a period of time invariably results in new challenges. In most instances a person either grows or deteriorates, and the crisis points are where either growth or deterioration can occur.

Frances listened attentively and concurred that this had indeed been the case. She was able to see she was now functioning at a much higher level, both as a mother and as a physician. She sighed, "But this is a painful process."

"Of course, it is," the therapist responded. "Remember, our mothers used to refer to growing pains. Growth is very often painful."

"How long do I have to keep on growing?" Frances asked.

"A person should hope to continue growing until death," the therapist said. "Because when you stop growing, you are likely to regress."

The episodic panicky calls stopped. Now, many years later, Frances admits she still has crises, and although they are often difficult, she no longer feels overwhelmed by them.

She works her A.A. program and has been able to use the program to help her through the rough spots.

I once came across a fascinating description of how lobsters grow. The lobster, encased in a hard, unyielding shell, grows to a point where the shell becomes very restrictive and stifling. It then retreats to a sheltered place, sheds its shell, and gradually forms a new one. This process is repeated numerous times until the lobster reaches its maximum size. Each time the lobster sheds its shell, even in the safety of its retreat, it is nevertheless at the mercy of sudden currents of water or predatory fish. The outer shell is its protective armor, and when it temporarily loses this defense it becomes vulnerable. Yet, in order to grow, the lobster must take such risks.

Growth and personality development in the human show many similarities with the lobster. If we don't grow, we remain stifled in a restrictive shell. Yet growth is not without various risks, and we are vulnerable in our growth phases. And just as the lobster must repeatedly expose itself to risks, so we humans must endure repeated episodes of some difficulties in our growth.

It is understandable that when we experience discomfort, we would like immediate relief. Indeed, the lack of tolerance for discomfort and the desire for immediate gratification are quite characteristic of alcoholism.

It is unrealistic to expect many years of low self-esteem to be undone and reversed in a brief period of time. The person who spends several weeks in a rehabilitation center and then has a period of sobriety in A.A. may be disappointed to still find depressive and self-depreciating feelings. It is important to realize that acquisition of a positive self-esteem may take many months or years.

The following letter from a recovering alcoholic states this very clearly.

"It was four years ago this month that I was taken into your office utterly beaten, wanting to die but without the courage to take my own life—so sick both mentally and spiritually. You were the only person who I would listen to—I knew you understood. Thanks to you I went back to A.A. and I made it through those first two years. Looking back, I can see how sick I was when I thought I was doing just fine. I remember how I would save up all my thoughts and feelings until I saw you again. The only thing I did right those first two years was not drink and go to meetings.

"I want you to know it has taken me four years to finally feel good about myself—to feel I have something to offer other people. I don't have to keep tearing myself down any more—I don't have to keep myself sick any more. Words can't express how I feel. I am just so grateful to my God, the program, and the people."

It is evident that conquering low self-esteem is not a one-time thing, but an ongoing process. This is reflected in the Tenth Step of the A.A. program, "We *continued* to take personal inventory. . . ." This is also what I mentioned previously in Chapter XV, that surrender is not a one-time event, but continues to grow in quality as the sense of self-esteem progressively improves.

Another trait often found in individuals with poor self-esteem is a difficulty or inability to accept legitimate help. The feeling of being unworthy and undeserving can generate intense discomfort and even guilt when help is accepted from another. This refusal to accept help, whether due to the feeling of being undeserving or believing "I can do it alone," may result in unnecessary suffering during recovery.

During a severe frigid weather spell, one young woman in the early phases of recovery slept in her icy apartment for several days while waiting for the furnace to be repaired. She would have been more than welcome at the homes of many friends, but was unable to ask for this simple help. More commonly encountered is the person who lacks means of transportation and is reluctant to call other members for rides to A.A. meetings, which would gladly be offered.

This hesitancy in accepting legitimate help should be a focus for those providing counseling to the alcoholic. The false pride that is characteristic of the active alcoholic needs to be eliminated in recovery, and growth should be characterized by a true pride in oneself.

CHAPTER XIX

GOALS AND PURPOSE

Whether drinking is compulsive or an escape from what the alcoholic perceives to be intolerable feelings, the active drinker's life is spent trying to feel good. Many recovering alcoholics attest that they did not drink for the taste nor to get high, but simply to feel normal. In fact, trying to feel normal becomes a prime goal in life.

In virtually every area of life, things have value because of their function. Homes have value as places to live in, automobiles for their ability to transport, instruments for the particular task for which they are designed, and art has its aesthetic value for its ability to please the eye or ear. If one were to have a highly complex piece of equipment composed of sophisticated machinery, but it couldn't do anything and had no conceivable function, it would be of no value to anyone.

One of the major ingredients of positive self-esteem is a sense of purpose in life. Purposelessness is a most deflating sensation.

Everybody has different goals or sense of purpose. People with religious convictions may believe that human life has value because it's divinely endowed, and that there is sanctity to human life. Others may believe there's no divine intervention and their goals and purposes are derived from their particular beliefs. But in order for a sense of purpose to have any meaning, the person must somehow adhere to it and realize it is of little value if it's merely an abstraction.

Active alcoholics who spend their lives just trying to feel normal, and achieve this only with the mind-blunting effect of alcohol, don't have the opportunity to pursue any other goal or purpose. There's nothing beyond this self-directed goal, and this is hardly satisfying.

One of the most important discoveries in recovery can be summarized in words we often hear from the alcoholic undergoing detoxification. "There's got to be more to life than this." Once the vicious cycle of drinking is eliminated and the brain begins to function more efficiently, the alcoholic can begin focusing on a sense of purpose or a goal in life.

A sense of purpose in life can be central to recovery. It's unlikely that a person will tolerate distress without good reason, but it's quite possible that a person will sacrifice for a higher principle. When the alcoholic experiences distress and knows alcohol will relieve it at least temporarily, having a sense of purpose other than just feeling good can help overcome the temptation to drink.

This sense of purpose may well be the "spiritual awakening" of which Alcoholics Anonymous speaks. The spiritual awakening is a most private experience and means different things to different people. It may or may not be religiously oriented. The important point is that the person recognizes there is a spiritual component to one's life, and there's more to life than simply seeking physical well-being.

Above and beyond the private spiritual awakening, the recovering alcoholic acquires an additional goal in life: a mission to help others out of the hell of active alcoholism. If a newly-recovering person walks into an A.A. meeting and sees 42 people who have stopped drinking, are functioning well, and experiencing some joy in life, he or she has

42 inspirations to encourage trying sobriety. If he or she sees 43 people who are sober at the meeting, then there are 43 sources of encouragement. The greater the sources of encouragement, the less difficult the struggle towards sobriety becomes. Just being sober, even without doing anything, becomes a source of inspiration and strength to others. For the recovering alcoholic, life takes on a new meaning, which may actually surpass the sense of purpose attainable by the nonalcoholic or the nondrinker.

As a first-year psychiatric resident, I was assigned to the walk-in clinic. One day a woman came in asking for help. The woman gave the high points of her history. When she was 24, married, and with a baby, she was drinking so heavily that her husband asked for a divorce. Recognizing that she was not fulfilling her functions as a wife and mother, she gave her husband the divorce and custody of the child. Free of all restraints, she now indulged in alcohol even more heavily.

Even at 61, when I first met her, Isabel was an attractive woman. She must have been stunning in her younger years, when she was much sought after as a companion, being wined and dined by the socially elite. As the years went on and alcohol took its toll, Isabel's social life deteriorated drastically. Between the ages of 30 and 57, she had more than 65 hospitalizations for "drying out." Her behavior had become so intolerable that her family eventually detached themselves completely from her, even refusing to respond to calls from the hospital. She made several token visits to Alcoholics Anonymous, but she never took the program seriously. Eventually she ended up in the skid-row flophouses.

At age 57, Isabel called a lawyer who had extricated her from many difficulties and asked him for a favor.

"What is it this time?" the lawyer asked.

"I want you to put me away in the state hospital for

a year," Isabel answered. (At that time, the Pennsylvania State Inebriate Act provided commitment for a period of one year for alcoholism.)

"You don't know what you're saying," the lawyer said. But as Isabel persisted, he suggested, "Think it over a while. If you still want it, I'll do it for you."

One week later, Isabel again asked for commitment to the state hospital which the lawyer then arranged. After the year of hospitalization was over, Isabel joined A.A. and took a job as a housekeeper.

At the time she consulted me, Isabel had been sober for four years. Her attempts to recontact her family had all been rejected. I was unable to determine just what it was that she was seeking in psychiatric help, but her story fascinated me. Obviously there had to be a motivating factor for her becoming sober and remaining sober even after being rejected by her family. Just what did she have to gain by becoming sober? Although I didn't see any need for treatment, I encouraged Isabel to return so that I could discover the reason for her sobriety.

Having learned nothing about alcoholism in medical school nor in my psychiatric training, I assumed, like many others, that alcoholism couldn't be treated. As the sessions with Isabel continued, I became aware of the workings of A.A. and was curious to attend the meetings of this group of people who treated a condition in ways of which medicine was apparently ignorant. The more I attended A.A., the more I found its basic philosophy is applicable to stress management, even when alcohol isn't involved.

Isabel's motivation for sobriety continued to elude me, and although I continued to see her until her death at 74, I never did discover any specific reason for her turning her life around. All I can conclude is that within every person there is self-respect and dignity which, no matter how deeply concealed, exists obstinately. There comes a time when a person discovers she dare not be anything less than she can be, and at such a time, the miracle of sobriety can occur.

Isabel's spiritual awakening may well have been a moment of awareness of her self-respect and dignity. Perhaps her goal in life was to be a truly dignified human being. Like any other seed, this was nurtured and grew into a beautiful living plant.

CHAPTER XX

SPIRITUALITY

Spirituality is of great importance and is one of the major self-realizations in recovery. It is worth elaborating upon even at the risk of repeating some points already stated.

I underwent psychiatric training at a time when medical science was just ushering in mood-altering drugs. Quite a revolution occurred with the introduction of the anti-psychotic drug, Thorazine, and, somewhat later, what were referred to as the "minor tranquilizers" such as Miltown and Librium. These latter drugs seemed to fulfill the promise of "tranquil but alert." At that time the addictive nature of the tranquilizers had not yet been noted.

I recall one day I felt very fortunate to be entering psychiatry after such a breakthrough in pharmacology. There was every indication that medical science could make available a safe "happy pill." We would now have the means to eliminate all emotional discomfort and make everyone content.

I was thinking this way while paging through a family magazine, and suddenly my eye caught an advertisement wherein a milk company boasted that its milk came from "contented cows." I paused a moment in what was to be for me a kind of awakening. If it were indeed possible to administer medication to make everyone content, was that the goal I should be pursuing? If this advertisement were correct, then the finest milk is given by contented cows, because obviously the finest cow is a contented cow. Contentment is then the ideal goal for a cow. Is the same to be said of human beings? Is there nothing more to which the human should aspire than to be content, a goal that can be shared with a cow?

Let us turn now to my definition of spirituality. I believe there are essentially three categories of animate beings: animals, angels, and humans. It stands to reason that if God had wanted any more of any one kind, He would have created them that way, and since He did not do so, each being must be what it was intended to be.

Animals are beings that function with instinct, avoiding harmful things. Animals go after whatever they crave, their only deterrent being pain or the threat of pain. Angels are the opposite of animals. They are pure spirit. They have no drives nor desires. They do what they are instructed to do. Human beings are composite beings. They are very much animal in body, and thus have all the impulses, drives, and cravings of an animal. However, we are different from other animals in that we have a spirit, an ability to develop a mastery over our animal bodies.

When a person refrains from doing something because a given act will elicit punishment, one is functioning at an animal level because an animal, too, will avoid doing something which it knows will result in punishment. It makes no difference whether the punishment consists of physical pain, incarceration, financial loss, or social disapproval. Restraint because of punishment is essentially animal in nature.

When the person develops a sense of right and wrong, life is directed according to principles and values which would not be transgressed even if there were no punitive consequences, even if the act were unknown to any other human. Then the person exercises a self-mastery which emanates from the spirit within. This is one phase of spirituality.

Another aspect of spirituality, as I understand it, is that rather than being a thing or an entity, spirituality is a process. One never attains spirituality, but rather constantly works at it. In fact, not only is it not attainable as a well-defined end point, but quite the contrary, the end point appears to progressively retreat.

The theologian Baal Shem Tov, founder of the Hasidic movement, was once consulted by one of his students who complained of severe frustration. It appeared to the student that the harder he strove to achieve a closeness to God, the more distant he was from his goal.

The teacher then responded with the following example: Suppose a father wishes to teach his infant child how to walk. He waits until the child is capable of standing upright, and the father then places himself very close to the child, perhaps a foot away, holds out his hands, and beckons the child to come. The child, wishing to reach the father, and seeing the supportive hands so close to him, has the courage to take the first tiny step. If the father were to embrace the child at this point, the skill in walking would not be achieved. Instead, the father immediately jumps back a bit, perhaps two feet away, and again beckons to the child. The child, having successfully taken the first step and seeing the father still very near to him, ventures another step or two. Again the father retreats and continues doing so until the child learns how to walk independently.

If we were able to read the child's mind, we would undoubtedly find him to be most frustrated. Although he continues making efforts to reach the father, it appears that the harder he tries, the more distant from him his father becomes. What is happening here is that there are two divergent goals. The goal of the child is to reach the father; however, the goal of the father is to teach the child how to walk independently. The father could embrace the child at any point and thereby satisfy the child's quest, but that would abort the learning process. The only way that the latter can proceed is for the goal to continue to retreat, to stimulate the child to walk.

This is true of spirituality, which is a constant growth process. Once we feel we have finally achieved spirituality, we have probably lost it. If we constantly strive toward self-mastery, self-improvement, and establishing higher goals for self, with a sense of at least a bit of frustration, we may feel that we're on the right track.

Understood as a process, spirituality has its frustrations because not only do we never arrive at an end point, but quite the contrary, the end point appears to progressively recede. In this sense, we can't ever become totally content. We can be happy in the knowledge that we are on the right track, but contentment and frustration are mutually exclusive.

In active alcoholism, the drinker seeks contentment, and this is temporarily provided by the alcohol anesthetic. It is not a true contentment such as a cow might experience, but rather an absence of awareness of any discomfort. There can be no awareness of discomfort if one is sufficiently anesthetized.

During active drinking, alcoholics cannot see themselves as spiritual beings. By definition, they are functioning at an animal level. In moments of clarity, they may realize they are really operating at a sub-human level, and this contributes very little to positive self-esteem. As sobriety begins and progresses and alcoholics become aware of an ability to achieve mastery, not only over the impulse to drink but also over many other drives, they can begin to appreciate themselves as spiritual human beings, a discovery which significantly promotes self-esteem. They can become aware that, whereas frustration and contentment are mutually exclusive, frustration and happiness are quite compatible. One can actually be happy while also being frustrated if he or she is aware that frustration often accompanies an active growth process, and there is joy in the realization that one is constantly undergoing the process of self-improvement.

CHAPTER XXI

PITFALLS IN RECOVERY

As wonderful as self-discovery is, it is not completely without pitfalls. The first risk is a relatively minor one. Self-discovery can be an elating experience. The newly-recovering alcoholic who for the first time in years has clarity in thought and an efficiently functioning brain may feel exhilarated. As self doubts are overcome and confidence gained, a recovering person may feel like someone freed after years of captivity.

This exhilarating feeling can backfire if the person now feels so self-confident and thinks that with newly discovered strength, he or she no longer needs involvement in A.A. Or he or she may think this newly emerged super human can now control what was previously uncontrollable and try drinking again. This is not self-discovery but self-deception. Unfortunately, this person's self-deception is likely to be set straight by a relapse into destructive drinking.

Another possible consequence is that this exhilaration of self-discovery may be quite intense in its early stages. It is like the novelty of having a new car, a feeling which soon fades away. The recovering alcoholic, who may have accumulated many aggravating problems while drinking, may feel so elated in the newly found sobriety and newly discovered self that this euphoria obscures the multitude of problems which still need to be confronted. But like every novelty, this, too, eventually loses its glamour, and the alcoholic may then experience a sudden letdown. This is a high risk period for relapse, and avoidance of this pitfall requires consistent involvement in recovery, with A.A. and qualified counseling.

The combination of the above two factors is especially dangerous, and one of the frequent causes of relapse. That is, the recovering alcoholic feels so enthused about the new self that the person feels he or she can go it alone and falls away from A.A., only to be hit by the depression that ensues when the novelty wears off. This is a one-two punch that often results in recurrence in drinking.

There is another pitfall which is more subtle and relevant to the future of an alcoholic marriage. The word "rehabilitation" is often used in regard to the treatment of alcoholics. There is a subtle issue here which needs to be clarified. When used in reference to a physical problem, such as the paralysis of an arm or leg following an accident, rehabilitation is clearly appropriate. The arm or leg had been healthy and functioning well until the time of the accident, and the goal of treatment is to return the limb to its pre-accident condition.

This is not true of alcoholism. Returning the person to the state prior to developing alcoholism is hardly an accomplishment. Obviously, the person progressed from the pre-alcoholic condition into active alcoholism. Recovery therefore must consist of helping the individual become a different person than before. A recovering alcoholic with over 25 years of sobriety said it very well. "The man I was drank, and the man I was will drink again."

The fact that the recovering alcoholic must develop a totally new personality may give rise to some problems. Suppose John and Jane meet and fall in love. John is 25; Jane is 22. They decide to marry. It is safe to assume that John and Jane found in each other that which each feels he or she needs for happiness. Now assume John develops a drinking problem, and at age 32 his alcoholism is severe enough to bring him into treatment. He enters a recovery program and works diligently on his sobriety.

John's personality begins to change as he works the Steps and gains insight. He begins to discover his real self. He develops a better self-image and may become more confident and self-assertive. Perhaps he used to allow others to make decisions because he was too insecure about his own decision-making capacity. This begins to change. Perhaps he used to try to please everyone because he was afraid of losing their friendship. This, too, begins to change. Perhaps he was overly dependent upon others, and now becomes more self-reliant.

A new John emerges. Not only a John that is different from the drinking John, but a John that is different from the pre-drinking John, the one that Jane fell in love with because he met her needs. Is it possible that the new John, although a thousand percent improved over the old John, is not what Jane had sought as a husband? If Jane remains stagnant and John continues to grow, the disparity between the two may become great and they may find themselves incompatible.

Sobriety can be a major growth phenomenon. If the nondrinking spouse doesn't participate in a growth program, the marriage may fail. It's understandable why some marriages which survive the drinking may fail after sobriety has been achieved.

If, however, Jane becomes involved in Al-Anon or in some other way promotes her own personality growth to keep pace with John, the marriage will not only survive, but become a very rich and rewarding relationship as both partners enjoy self-discovery and growth.

CHAPTER XXII

PSYCHOTHERAPY AND COUNSELING

It has been estimated that, in perhaps eighty percent of all cases, alcoholism is primary; that is, it is the disease, and not a reaction to stress, depression, or whatever else. However, in twenty percent of the cases, it is felt that the person began drinking as a response to some sort of emotional problem. Even in many of the latter cases, the alcoholism often attains a life of its own, and might well continue even if the underlying problem is eliminated. By the same token, in these latter twenty percent, it is unlikely the drinking will stop unless the underlying problem is eliminated. Among these cases may be those drinkers who failed to stop drinking in spite of their A.A. involvement. A.A. recognizes this when it states that there are some people who don't appear able to give themselves over to the program.

It is a simple observation that in those eighty percent where alcoholism is primary, treating it as though it were symptomatic is going to be unsuccessful. Conversely, when the alcoholism is secondary to an underlying problem, ignoring the latter may result in failure. Of course, the overwhelming support provided the A.A. fellowship and personality changes brought about by working the Twelve Steps may be sufficient to bring about recovery even in secondary or symptomatic alcoholism. It is also possible that addressing the underlying problem in the latter cases may be essential.

It's unfortunate that alcoholism hasn't been properly or sufficiently taught in many professional schools relating to human services. Speaking from my own experience, I was taught nothing about alcoholism in four years of medical school. Even in three years of intensive study of psychiatry I learned nothing about alcoholism. This leads me to suspect that many physicians and psychiatrists currently practicing medicine and psychiatry are still unfamiliar with the disease. This is likely true of many other therapists as well. Unless these professionals have made an effort to acquire expertise, they're incapable of adequately examining for alcoholism, making a correct diagnosis, and instituting proper treatment.

Many physicians don't know how to take a history regarding alcoholism. As with other illnesses, they're likely to rely on information provided by the patient. With alcoholism this is often absolutely worthless, since the alcoholic rarely tells the truth about alcohol consumption and what effect alcohol has. A patient may tell the doctor that he or she drinks "socially" even though a fifth of liquor is consumed daily, or its equivalent in beer. Whether the alcoholic is willfully lying or unconsciously denying, the doctor doesn't get the true facts, yet operates on the assumption that they were.

In instances where alcoholism is blatant and there is gross physical evidence of alcohol excess, some physicians will advise the patient to "cut down" on drinking, not realizing that it is beyond the patient's ability to do so. They may refrain from telling the patient the correct diagnosis of alcoholism because they don't want to offend him or her. They may accept the person's sincere promise not to drink again as having some substance, whereas in fact it's meaningless.

Many psychiatrists who don't recognize the primary character of alcoholism are apt to approach its treatment as any other emotionally based symptom, by trying to get at the psychological origin of the problem. In these cases, the patient continues to visit the doctor regularly and talk about childhood experiences and relationships to significant others while continuing to consume alcohol. Nothing of merit can ever result from this course. Others may prescribe tranquilizers which can be just as addictive as the alcohol, and which the alcoholic may even combine with drinking and get dangerous results. Some psychiatrists, noting the depression manifested by almost every alcoholic, will attempt to treat this depression with anti-depressant medications. These are of little value when the depression is secondary to the alcoholism and aren't effective in a brain that is saturated with alcohol.

Because of the lack of understanding about alcoholism among many professionals and the resultant improper treatment, many people in Alcoholics Anonymous assume all health professionals are inept in treating the alcoholic, that no alcoholic should ever receive psychiatric medications of any kind, and that no formal psychotherapy should ever be done with the alcoholic.

This error is no less serious than those of the inadequately trained professionals. There are physicians, psychiatrists, and psychotherapists who have a good understanding of alcoholism; there are some alcoholics who require psychotherapy for a successful recovery, and there are some alcoholics who may need appropriate psychiatric medication. The crucial point is that a proper evaluation must be performed by someone qualified in alcoholism and in the diagnosis and treatment of emotional illnesses.

Many depressive illnesses are the consequence of some bodily change wherein there's an upset in the body's neurohormones (hormones acting on nervous tissue). Just as some physiologic disorders can produce symptoms of the digestive or respiratory systems, there are some disorders that produce symptoms of the emotional apparatus, that manifest themselves as depression. In depression, there's frequently a deep sense of worthlessness along with various other symptoms. This particular sense of low self-esteem won't likely improve until the body chemistry is corrected, whether spontaneously or with the help of anti-depressant medication.

Just as alcoholics are vulnerable to pneumonia or diabetes, so are they vulnerable to a biochemically induced depression. This depression is different from that so often encountered in alcoholics, where depression is the result of alcoholism.

Just as it is a mistake to prescribe medications for depressions that are secondary to alcoholism, so is it a mistake to deny anti-depressant medication to alcoholics who have a biochemical disease that is not a consequence of drinking.

A similar occurrence is that in manic attacks. In this disorder, a patient may become grandiose, hyperactive, and apt to do many bizarre things which are similar to what a person may do when judgment is impaired by alcohol. A striking example of this is a woman who had multiple hospitalizations for detoxification, sometimes separated by several months of abstinence. Periodically, she would become very loud and hyperactive, and would cause such disturbances at A.A. meetings that she was asked to leave. At her last detoxification, it was suspected that she had recurrent manic attacks, and that it was during these episodes that she drank uncontrollably. She was treated with Lithium, which is a medication that often prevents occurrences of manic attacks. She hasn't had a recurrence of either manic behavior or drinking for the past eleven years, and remains active in A.A.

It was because of cases like this that some investigators considered Lithium as a possible treatment for alcoholism. It's my feeling that Lithium is ineffective in treating alcoholism except for those cases where there's a mood disorder independent of the alcohol problem. It would be just as wrong not to use Lithium in these occasional cases as it would be to use it for every hyperactive alcoholic.

Just as there are some instances where pharmacological treatment is necessary, there are also cases where psychotherapy is helpful. It's wise not to initiate in-depth psychotherapy until there has been a long period of complete abstinence to allow the mind to be totally clear of alcohol influence, and for the person to return to a more normal behavior. It's possible that many emotional problems may become totally resolved just by maintenance of sobriety, and a delay of at least six months, perhaps sometimes even up to two years, would be wise before initiating in-depth psychotherapy. Until this time, psychotherapy is best to be of the supportive variety, helping the individual adjust to and cope with current reality problems.

It's absolutely crucial that psychotherapy for the recovering alcoholic who is involved with A.A. be conducted by a therapist who understands alcoholism and is familiar with the A.A. program. Psychotherapy and A.A. working at cross purposes can be very harmful to the recovering alcoholic. The therapist who is familiar with how A.A. works and how the patient is working the program can be of immense help to the recovering alcoholic who has some psychological obstacles that impede recovery.

It's essential that professionals who provide services to the alcoholic receive adequate training in the understanding of this disease. Since A.A. is the most effective method of attaining and maintaining sobriety, professionals should be knowledgeable in its operation. It's also essential for those in the A.A. community to recognize that there are emotional disorders not caused by alcohol, that the alcoholic, like the nonalcoholic, is vulnerable to these, and that treatment by a professional who is well trained in alcoholism is not incompatible with participation in Alcoholics Anonymous.

CHAPTER XXIII

SELF-DISCOVERY AND RELAXATION

Many people think stress and tension cause alcoholism. This is not accurate because there are countless people who suffer from a great deal of stress and tension who aren't alcoholic. Furthermore, there are many alcoholics who don't appear to be victims of any particularly severe stress and tension. However, stress and tension can aggravate the alcoholic's drinking and are particularly of concern to the recovering alcoholic, who is at risk of relapsing into drinking to escape tension. It's therefore important for the recovering alcoholic to develop ways of coping with tension other than by anesthetizing with alcohol.

Stress and tension can come from various sources and, contrary to popular belief, not all stress is harmful. There are many instances when a person is confronted by a challenge and is under stress and can't relax until the challenge is resolved. In these situations, the stress is clearly identifiable, well defined, and of relatively brief duration. These kinds of stress are not only harmless, but are actually often constructive. It's when the person can't identify or clearly define the source of tension and when it's indeterminate in duration that it becomes intolerable. The tension may lead to many unhealthy reactions, among which is the possibility of escaping into the oblivion of alcohol intoxication.

Tension and relaxation are opposites and mutually exclusive. They can't coexist in the same person. Relaxation is thus the natural antidote to tension, and when achieved, can eliminate tension.

Many people believe they know how to relax, but a closer analysis reveals this is often not so. What is generally considered relaxation is only diversion. Most people are capable of diverting themselves, whether by watching television, playing golf, reading a book, playing cards, or the like, but not everyone is capable of true relaxation.

An example of true relaxation is the person who is lying on the beach, or sitting at the side of a swimming pool, eyes closed, absorbing the sun, doing nothing other than breathing, and enjoying this. Some people can do this very well, but many others find this intolerable for more than a few seconds. They must listen to a radio or read a book or otherwise divert themselves.

People who seek diversion are not always trying to distract themselves from external pressures and worries. Very often they are seeking to draw attention away from themselves. Without diversion or distraction of any kind, a person is left only with self; and when the person is discontented with self, he or she can't possibly enjoy relaxation. No one enjoys being in the company of someone he or she dislikes. The person who suffers from low self-esteem and dislikes self is incapable of true relaxation. If he or she can't divert self, the person is at great risk of escaping from the annoying company into the oblivion of alcohol.

Alcoholics who are mired in low self-esteem, both that which existed before drinking and that which resulted from the many ego-deflating consequences of drinking, and who try to abstain on their own, therefore have an additional factor which tends to abort abstinence. Alcoholics are not isolated by virtue of people having left them because they can't be tolerated. Alcoholics are terribly uncomfortable because they can't tolerate being with themselves. This inability to have moments of peace and tranquility often contributes to relapse.

Sometimes the abstaining alcoholic (often referred to as "dry but not sober") who has an inability to attain tranquility in relaxation, will try to escape by increasing diversionary activities. If the alcoholic has a job or business he or she may bring work home or expand business ventures. Temporarily, the alcoholic may become a workaholic, and may sometimes have successes to show for all the efforts. However, in the final analysis, one can't constantly run away from self. There's no way to be involved in diversionary activities 24 hours a day, seven days a week, and invariably this method fails. The confrontation with one's self re-emerges, and when workaholism fails, the alcoholism is apt to recur.

Recovering alcoholics who attain even rudimentary self-esteem in abstinence have a much better chance of success. The support of the A.A. fellowship and the evidence that others like themselves have achieved a sense of inner peace, enables them to better live with themselves. Early in recovery, the depth of the cumulative low self-esteem may make some moments of solitude a hellish experience, and some people may see recovering people running frequently to A.A. meetings or calling up other recovering alcoholics as nothing but another variety of diversion. While it can't be denied that participation in A.A. may also be diversionary, it's nevertheless an experience which contributes toward positive self-esteem, and surviving the next day becomes just a little bit easier.

Occasionally I hear criticism of recovery through A.A. as being merely the substitution of one dependency for another; that is, substituting dependency on Alcoholics Anonymous instead of on the bottle. The response to this is twofold. First of all, dependency on alcohol is obviously harmful. Alcoholic drinking is damaging to the brain, liver, and many other vital body organs. Alcoholic behavior is generally devastating not only to the alcoholic, but also to the family and employer. If A.A. were indeed only a substitute dependency, even its most severe critics would have to concede that it's a dependency which doesn't destroy nor impair the person's brain and vital organs, and one in which the person generally becomes more productive than ever before.

A second response is more philosophical. It's wrong to think humans can be totally self-sufficient and independent. For all our needs, physical, social, and psychological, we are all dependent on others. Absolute independence is a myth. A diabetic who is dependent on insulin for life adjusts to this dependency and can lead a very productive and satisfying life, in spite of an awareness that missing even a single day's dose of insulin could be serious and possibly fatal.

Yes, the alcoholic develops a dependence on A.A. to be saved from a malignant disease. No therapy has as yet come close to the effectiveness and success of A.A. There is reason to suspect that those who reject A.A. because it is a "substitute dependency" actually have other reasons for doing so, and the dependency criticism is nothing more than a rationalization.

The continuing need for A.A. involvement shouldn't detract from self-esteem any more than the need to maintain daily insulin treatment does for the diabetic. Diabetes and alcoholism are both chronic diseases, and recovering alcoholics, like well-controlled diabetics, can enjoy a very positive self-concept.

The personality growth and self-awareness acquired in recovery enables the alcoholic to emerge from a profound sense of low self-esteem to a very positive self-esteem. The recovering alcoholic then feels more content with self and can be at ease in his or her own company. The person can now relax and enjoy relaxation, and a major threat to relapse is greatly minimized.

CHAPTER XXIV

CHOICE AND RESPONSIBILITY

"Today I have a choice."

This statement is frequently heard in the narration of a recovering alcoholic.

Choice and responsibility are closely intertwined and characterize maturity. Small children and people who are grossly incompetent because of brain dysfunction aren't held responsible for their actions because they're considered completely impulse driven and without adequate capacity to make a choice or to exercise their free will.

The actively drinking alcoholic is somewhat akin in this respect to those who lack the capacity to choose, but is one who regains the capacity as his or her self is freed of alcohol domination. The words "somewhat akin" are deliberately chosen, because the active alcoholic can't be granted the immunity of a minor or a mentally disabled person. The alcoholic must be held responsible for all his or her actions, even those committed while intoxicated. This is essential not only for social survival, since a person can't be allowed to set up a defense for anti-social behavior simply by getting drunk, but also because allowing the alcoholic to consider him- or herself irresponsible would feed into the illness.

Active drinkers may go to absurd lengths to escape responsibility. They may contend that they are hopeless. This isn't because of a sense of despair, but rather because being incurable removes the burden of making an effort at recovery.

One young woman hospitalized for detoxification persistently pressed to have a brain scan and electroencephalogram performed because she thought she had suffered brain damage as a result of her drinking. Even though she was repeatedly reassured there was no clinical sign of any brain damage, her pleas continued. A closer analysis revealed that she actually wished to be diagnosed as brain damaged, because this would then allow her to regress into drinking. "You can't expect me to recover. I don't have the capacity. I'm brain damaged."

The issue of responsibility is thus central to sobriety and to the sense of maturity and self-esteem. In fact, the recovering alcoholic frequently has a sense of responsibility that surpasses that of the nonalcoholic or nondrinker.

It's interesting to observe many recovering alcoholics in their daily function. They will often exhibit a sense of responsibility far superior to that of the nonalcoholic in relationship to their families, friends, and God. I've seen some recovering alcoholics agonize over decisions which others would treat lightly, but to them it is an either/or phenomenon. Either they accept responsibility for all their behavior, or relinquish responsibility for everything.

Our abhorrence of slavery is due to an intense conviction that a human being should be free to master his or her own life and destiny. Enslavement by alcohol is no less repulsive than enslavement by a human master. The recovering alcoholic discovers that he or she is indeed free, and, as a fully mature person, is willing to accept the burden of making choices and to be responsible for them.

CHAPTER XXV

AWARENESS OF INTERNAL BEAUTY AND STRENGTH

Enhancing coping skills is essential in achieving and maintaining recovery from alcoholism. Many people who feel they are unable to cope are also prone to seek escape into the alcohol oblivion when confronted by various challenges. People can be helped to cope through instruction and guidance in dealing with particular circumstances. While this method is helpful, it leaves a great deal to be desired.

Assume we walk into a dark room which is familiar to me but strange to you. I take you by the hand and lead you around, pointing out each item in the room. Chances are you won't remember the layout of the room after one lesson, and you might require repeated guided tours. On the other hand, if I turn on a light so you can see everything in the room for yourself, you need no individual instruction, and your understanding of how to get about the room is much better than by the first method.

When the recovering alcoholic overcomes feelings of inadequacy and comes to appreciate his or her strengths and capabilities, there is no longer any need for instruction on coping with every single challenge. The light has been put on and the person can see his or her way around.

This shouldn't be taken to mean that, at some stage in recovery, the alcoholic is totally independent and can discontinue involvement in A.A. Experience has repeatedly demonstrated that drifting away from the program results in eventual relapse. Ongoing participation in A.A. is essential not only to promote continuing personality growth, but also to avoid re-emergence of the negative self-image, which is an ever-present threat.

So, to all those embarking on the road to recovery, as well as to those who are already enroute, *bon voyage!* The trip is an exciting one, although there are some hazardous obstacles. Along the way there's beauty to be admired, appreciated, and enjoyed, not only in the scenery along the road, but primarily and most importantly, within yourself.